Also by Wayne Koestenbaum

Ultramarine

marine

Nightboat Books
New York

Wayne Koestenbaum

Ultra-

ISBN 978-1-64362-115-9

Designed and composed by Crisis
Text set in Akzidenz and Didot

Cataloging-in-publication date is available
from the Library of Congress

Nightboat Books
New York
www.nightboat.org

for Steven Marchetti

Contents

Ultramarine

#1

[my prostate a shopping mall]

goodnight, new
year—I meant to begin
in Barbra's voice
but I'm speaking in my
own voice as Ralph Fiennes

——————

discussed the allure
of cadmium orange
at dim sum this
morning, also men-
tioned caput mortuum

——————

remembered M.'s
low-pitched speaking
voice and his Moses
hand on mine—could
I have pushed that friend-
ship more resolutely
in gay direction?

———————

why did I equate
words and genital sensation?

———————

I remain uncertain
about the function
of suppositories

———————

made a spontaneous
mark with a leftover tube
of auratic ultramarine,
finger-smeared it
to create abrupt
punctuating lines—

———————

squeezed Mars violet
and Persian rose into
crevices where ultramarine
remained visible
around embroidered
green-stained titanium buff

————

today I'm a puce
or carmine Barbra

————

longing to stop at San
Jose smoke shop to study
hypothesized smut

————

Saint-Saëns concerto
(signifying Agamemnon)
fed my wish to triangulate
with pale closeted pianist,
my handpicked Count
Almaviva and my
private Moses, ineligible
for the Mount

————

　　　as a woman
Moses apologized for
his girth

————

the backs of his upper
arms not my property

———————

young fops reading Edna
Ferber's *Show Boat* or *Giant*
don't flash organs
to older tourist guys

———————

small and smooth, my
prostate mistaken
for a shopping mall

———————

dreamt that Liz and Dick
in a theater's back row
watched a movie—
in profile Liz was
not beautiful

———————

why did Dick seem
the loser in this daisy-
pied arrangement?

————

      her discovery
of my cock began
to equal my own
apprehension of its
rumored existence

————

reclaim German citizenship

————

develop crush based
on his theft—smittenness
founded on Robin
Hood strategy of stealing
back my rightful property

————

several dead poets
chorally eviscerate my tie
to pansy riot

————

efface ocean and choose field—
encode flow *within* field

———————

mother ate tuna and read
War and Peace at Stickney's,
a circumstance I idolized

———————

       diplomat
at Jackie Onassis's book
party—Asia Society—
mistook me for chicken

———————

is it ethically fraudulent
to teach prison literature?

———————

inviting you to
ignite my ignorance

———————

what is third-person plural
pronoun (they) in Italian?
why can't I remember he

or she or it or they?
do Italian speakers
leave he or she
or it or they
unspoken and unspecified?

8

#2

[do-it-yourself placenta]

      waiting for Lohengrin
magic to reappear
Unter den Linden
twilight in Lehár

————

B-side of Nazism is Dresden
marching anti-immigration

————

      Polk
I can picture, also Folsom,
but not Tenderloin—
can I picture Locanda Montin
in Venice where I saw
James Merrill in 1985?

————

     naches,
a wandering speck
on snow

————————

closest companion
is my cough—I hug it

————————

  Marnie tabula
rasa like *Summertime*
with Kate Hepburn is my heart's
domain—*Red Sky*
at Morning with not John
Wayne but a pubarche boy

————————

saw lithograph of bearded lady
19th century, saw videos
of porn stars demonstrating
how to put on condoms

————————

gay hubbies who make
their goody-goody star wives
perform nude scenes

————————

Galina Gorchakova disappeared
after her San Diego *Norma*—
no one applauded her
big aria in *Don Carlo*—
a fan saw defeat on her face

—————

        Alva
Edison versus Alma Gluck,
 "va" and "ma" make
"vama"—vampire
minus the Magna Carta

—————

    why isn't smegma
more frequently discussed?

—————

    Irish Spring
cloaked boy smell

—————

    snow on jagged
rocks beneath logs, two
echelons of tree

———

can a twig
remaining on a tree
retain twig identity?

———

choose a eucalyptus or red-
wood for life and never deviate
to a different tree

———

train time is death
time, like *Magnificent Obsession*
gaping, showing its rah-rah nature—

———

a rah-rah is a conformist
but not the Bertolucci kind

———

say it aloud first and
then write it, voice chained
to transportation-poesy

———

Tabatha standing
on porch with urine-stained
underwear—dream espousing
witchcraft

_____

never taught
how to shave, a lost scene—
figuring masculinity out
by myself, and I never
figured it out

_____

Swiss toy monorail as Xmas
or Hanukkah offering,
boy-ecstasy folded in half

_____

don't brag
about exultation

_____

Branwell Brontë a drunk
and lech, Charlotte dead

in childbirth, excessive
vomiting—Gaskell
could have helped
Charlotte abort
because she wanted to write
another novel, not take
care of a kid

_____

      a gap
inside my placenta—
I teach myself digital-
anal placenta warfare

_____

why must hunger immediately
be satisfied?

_____

      GIs traumatized
by crematorium footage
studied law and physics,
Plato and geometry, taxation
and Thackeray

14

———

we wrote
guides to Rome and botched
our foreskins by redeeming
them at Blue Chip Stamp counters

———

crawling
turtle I remember you
dying on your brackish island—
did I kill my turtle? was it
my job to change its water?
turtle drying out on plastic
oasis above foul pond

———

I didn't love my
turtle—I recognized
its parsimonious distance
from human norms—
I, too, deviated
from personhood

———

the turtle beheld
my inhumanity

———————

    my coldness
sequestered me—a null interior
composed of self-generated
rudiments, my home-crafted
do-it-yourself placenta

———————

    eat more
rice says the Auschwitz
survivor but I
don't want more rice

———————

gay man's slow glide—
glide is a sexually
harassing word

———————

drawing is simply
tracing, discovering a void,

relearning how to find
shapes and narratives
in what had appeared
to be a void—look closely
at voids and they become
multitudinous

———————

         Anita
Ekberg died today is
another appetite suppressant

———————

I won't compliment his socks—
he already knows he's handsome
and doesn't need ego reinforcement

———————

a compulsion to appear more
masculine than he really is

———————

        in Berlin he fisted
a stranger, half the forearm

_____

no interest in fisting as
experience but much interest
in fisting as narrative

_____

I'm proud to be
German he says

_____

deprived of statehood, needing
to leave home because home
has turned against you

_____

why the Allies
didn't bomb the camps

_____

his beard
smears diapason on me

_____

if Icarus
dandles me

on knee carillon
listing toward
temporary unison

_____

who directs ass's
orchestra? can ass be
possessive? can ass conduct
an orchestra or be paid
for bandleading, and can I die
to become statistician or
neurologist of ass as seen by
Donna Reed suddenly in
camera obscura retrospect?

_____

driver this morning seemed
blind or with a segment
gouged out of his skull

_____

elegant wealthy woman
has a dungeon she

calls The Room,
white vinyl or rubber piss-
proof surface

————————

sacrilege is the Leonardo
DiCaprio word on my stomach
emblazoned

————————

oral suction in bris
gives herpes

————————

      want phlegm to
gather musically in my lungs

————————

kindergarten, Tommy Thomason,
was that his name?
his mucusy drippy
voice, a drooling capacity

————————

yard of house
where drooling
Tommy lived

_____

           what
part does his saliva-
rich mouth play in our
friendship? drooling
Tommy I try
to hold onto frail memory
of your excess moisture

_____

       dissonance
resolved of your rheumy
face suddenly
recognizing me

_____

Tommy Thomason,
likeness of first and last name
a sign of drool, first-
name energies splashing
onto last name

———————

mouth's in-dwelling liquor,
swishing it around
teeth and lips to find
secret merriment

———————

discover
other little Jewish boys
talkative as I

———————

man with residual
scar of corrected
cleft lip—I recognize
that amended place,
healed residue
softening the "t" when
he says "ten"

———————

fear
of the terminal hour
when wolf, barred
from human sleep, howls

———————

finality hits me
like a tenement—
on top of grazing
is the beast that grazes

#3

[speedy fruit with bubbles]

      Chez Butt,
angel blue sideways red
abstraction

_____

      loving the legacy
I create as relaxed
Czar or lazar, not
Lazarus but fractured
metaphorical leper

_____

dislike of two stray
dead hairs cut
on page's table

_____

      my tie
is too expensive the song
says but you can't
trust promiscuous lyrics

June Havoc Berlioz—
June Havoc demarcates
Berlioz, June Havoc
is demarcated by Berlioz,
or a plus-size Berlioz
is ultra-demarcated by
a bunch of June
Havocs, a cold June Havoc
warming up a fell
Berlioz, a fallen Berlioz
in love (backwards
chronologically) with
a plush June Havoc
learning to long for
her own ruined habitat
in Berlioz's eyes

----

heavy humid Schiele
in mist, she rinses
Schiele shortly, June
Havoc grammatically
rinses Schiele shortly,

the gay department of
Thursday's Schiele speaking
Italian to work-related
June Havoc, but specify
why June Havoc

———————

       suddenly
who is June Havoc from
the narrator's point
of view coming to ease
the blue stain

———————

he's chill with June Havoc
alive in a role mis-
begotten on hold,
June Havoc whole and
flowery, a high or hiked
June, like June took
a long hike up Yosemite's
tallest peak to try coming
alone up there novelistically
as what Berlioz took for granted

————————

speedy fruit with bubbles—
underwater plants with
celestial details

————————

who dominates? or does
no one dominate? and is
domination not the issue?

————————

reading Simone Weil,
wanting to find
the hurt, pocked portion
of being, afraid that
I possess a caved-in
plank that will open
a door onto incarnation
or simply passage-
way through pleats immortally
strewn along now's
highway—I'll faint
while falling into elixir's
or crime's cosmic crevice

_____

azure impaled
me in the nose—
my head an open
corridor or cement sluice

_____

seeing demolished Penn
Station from Jackie Onassis's
presumed point of view

_____

     Parker
Tyler next year I meant
Parker Posey overdetermining
Troy—

_____

     dreamt I gave
myself a long blow job,
then my mouth stank
of penis, my own—
wondered if people would
smell it, and would they know
it was my own stink?

————————

to my brethren I address
this playlet

————————

    snorting
supercilious heavy-breathing
gay guy browsing his Twitter

————————

    sempiternal
Corsican trek in hot
tight clothes then lying
down naked near necropolis

————————

unshaped carcass
progresses unpaced

————————

red neon letters advertising
a defunct bathroom

————————

creating a vibe while pretending
not to possess a vibe,
Agamemnon hit on me

—————

tuché = "the encounter with the real"

—————

      pregnant
lying-down sickroom shape
of water stains on tablecloth—
specter my sickness matches

—————

to be greased and cradled,
underage unclaimed
waiting in a photographed
void to consider
repetition a friend
dwelling in corners
disowned—your impersonal tone

—————

      sequential
marks laid down

obedient to language's
stacking decree—words
must be stacked,
parts arranged and tabulated

———————

rhetoric, my fake Lowell
Apollonian Delmore
Schwartz side?

———————

please invent a more
forgiving regime of book

———————

      I said "snowfall-
as-erasure" in email
to handsome photographer—
afraid he'll think I was
aiming to erase him
rather than trying to praise
the palpable erasures pop-
ulating his abstract tableaux

#4

[egg hat]

start taking
Pepto-Bismol for the sake
of post-bop joy

———————

in Claude Chabrol's *Violette,*
Stéphane Audran is exigent
erotomaniacal mother in mode
of Delphine Seyrig's Jeanne Dielman
despising her own
libido and placing towel
under body to absorb
intercourse leakage

———————

filthy
sandwiches attached
to my egg hat's
microscript are the only
solution to censorship

————

      Frankenstein's monster
lurches toward Thornfield—
Prometheus sees me
with anaclitic gaze, Nosferatu
Kinski snake
daughter teeth

————

      isn't art
a transcendent category?

————

Jean Harris allegedly
murdered Scarsdale
diet doctor Tarnower
in state of jealous rage
fueled by amphetamine
withdrawal and did
penance in prison

————

      he went S/M
in Chicago and converted

to evangelical Christianity,
repentance for sex-club binge—
fucked in a sling?

————————

    drop him if he
proves a sluggish interlocutor
about desired butt curvature

————————

    OK experimental
patient describe
your visions—eyes closed
I see a forest
summoning many
trees into unity

————————

    Raskolnikov
Buddha has plaque
and hallucinates a squash
shirt, preferable to a plum

————————

when did you have
sex with a man for
the first time I asked

_____

contemplate silent acts
of deliberate composition
as opposed to garrulous
unboundaried confraternity

_____

emcee kicks folding
chairs and doesn't greet me

_____

pounding
his hero-chest like exiled
Russian prince bewailing
Glenn Gould mother-*praeludium*

_____

embargo on my
name, criminality
inside its feminine

habit or un-
feminine is
less criminal
and masculine is a
sick and ending pose,
masculinity a thing
to be extirpated,
unrhymed mascu-
linity in bop
frequency or
post-masculine pre-
bop orgasmic
dysfunction
within metaphor's
sepia giving
me away

———————

    avoid
participating as Barbara
Bel Geddes Midge—
any Midge-identified actions
are difficult, but if I focus
too much on Tyranno-

saurus rex or involve
Tippi Hedren, I'll fail

_____

       Xmas
stollen is gay,
touch it,
sweater queen,
touch varieties of
sweater queen, touch
inadequacy and in-
accuracy of his household
zippered-velvet intercrural
frottage escutcheon—

_____

       focus on a
childhood memory like
glue pots I feared
and failed to master,
board game Clue
like cosmic Herb
Alpert tinnitus or
titanium-white *Sextette*

Mae West teeth on
Herb Alpert's girlfriend
and John Berryman's suicide
relevant to this
sweaty turquoise thread,
a threat of Herb Alpert
making inroads on Psyche's
kosher chicken religious
experience long
vowel stuffed with rosemary

#5

[pretzel stick's proximity to nothingness]

       embarrassed to read
Coma because he'll ask
is your mother in a coma?
why are you curious
about comas? do you want
to fall into a coma?

————————

too noisy with brides here to read
Anne Carson's translated *Hekabe*

————————

       braggarts
with beards accept leaks
in the stained city—
pretzel stick in stubble mouth

————————

       mourning
the consoler I turned

my face toward the
Julie I begged to yell

_____

outer edge
of the body is too soft—be
concrete, cloaked by Odysseus
shadow of inhibition, a son
with stuffed nose versus
a father with stuffed nose

_____

willow *salce* crying
because husband Otello will kill
unusually sweet
pickle forging a new breast in me—
can a breast be *inside* me?

_____

etwas implies torture of
consecutive language—
I stare simply to joust

_____

in elevator
see nipples through his shirt,
touch chest and drag
hand downward
lightly like swiping
a credit card

———————

dank theater's double feature
Carousel and *King and I*—
"Saratoga Theater
smells like a toilet"
mother complained—
toilet smell didn't deter me
from matinee bliss

———————

did coffee
burn on girl's leg
("my father spilled
hot coffee on me") signal
abuse? stained
leg of little girl next door
with drooling brother

forced to pick up
dog shit in cold
birthday backyard—
indignity of handling
dried turds on festal morn

_____

      Iago is
cruel and homosexual,
but Iago is lake and
madness like Lucia
regnava nel
silenzio you stare mad
into a pond

_____

words poured into the fosse
—is force of falling
words a reparative use
of gravity?

_____

dreamt he called and said
I have good news and bad

news—I can't remember
the good but the bad
news was that she
had committed suicide

———————

when we beseech
square-jawed taciturnity
we don't know what erotic
bulwark we are beseeching

———————

memory of his teacher's
gray skirt or kangaroo
kindness pouch—
"Waltzing Matilda"
she taught them to sing

———————

first-grade Janice's
alluring sty area
reddened below one eye

———————

43

did sty come from a father-
induced injury?
are notebooks injurious?

————————

when I tried to praise
his cheekbones and skull
he stemmed my onrush

————————

enjoying proximity
to nothingness,
afraid of tendency to speak
in psychotic shorthand

————————

my slack face hacked
into permanent smile-grimace

————————

dreamt poet in underwear
by coffee table gave me a secret
posthumous message from Robert
Ashley but didn't decipher it

————————

go back in time to
degraded blue suit
pants on dirty john
floor, walking home
saying I worship your
cock—*frites* failure
to utilize his
ass appropriately

————————

he said our cocks look
alike, but was his
infinitesimally bigger?

————————

I mentioned biocock
in class—how many teachers
mention biocock
with impunity?

————————

            staring
flirtatiously at tall

grumpy man the year
discourse shut down

----

driving to P-town
snow-clad beach in
dream repeatedly
a roller coaster among
other vehicles responsible
for my welfare, my
destruction of wheat
and tares as I send
my Christianity to the
dump and acquire
Thomas Aquinas speed

----

reading the vagina
paper's shock value
in claustral Branwell
Brontë library's
glyph-gulf

----

suicide today (belt
or thread?) of death
row man awaiting execution

_____

a good word
to end or begin
your book is *syphilis*

#6

[art's marsupial pouch]

    grandfather
loving passé British
writers—Masefield

————————

beard wen smoke funk
nap in T-shirt—
bowties I borrow,
Traviata Toscanini
album in shame
breakfront with Jan
Peerce Passover LP

————————

tattooed guy ordered
three-dollar prosciutto
chunk like a steak
slab with pickles

————————

plinth beneath Assyrian
statue ISIS
smashed—anger of he
who smashes antiquity

————————

Leonard Nimoy died

————————

      Harriet the Spy
taking notes on cruel neighbor-
girl in Hallmark store
near Westgate mall, greeting
cards *Sandpiper*-epochal

————————

Bradley Cooper's
uterine incapacity—
Bradley reads
this notebook and laughs
alive in a world not be-
longing to me

————————

sober orange trousers
mom wardrobe
sugar-overdosing

_____

      dizzy nest
of wens to signify
fatal talismanic
admiration of
hirsute oratory

_____

excretory demandingness
is anal rage or
art's marsupial pouch

_____

      my aunt
loving Papageno's
crummy amok
majority

_____

lobster
roll in a paper bag,
clove-scented Reuben

———————

pregnant
blister on thumb-
fringe from badly-
handled suitcase

———————

invites me
to aleatory apartment,
shower together
on 100th anniversary
of Schwarzkopf's birth

———————

eat hamantaschen
without knowing
their function or meaning

———————

hey
Mélisande where are
you going, I miss
you, mystic Mé-
lisande, why
do I hug
my smallness?

_____

rebellion
against poet who used
"word salad" as slur

_____

music unfolds
upon sloping
Mephistopheles

_____

original sin I said
was in my DNA

_____

applauded her keen
phrase "lesbian judgment"

    _____

anges
purs, anges
radieux, Faust
concavity I occupy
when I explain
the spanked boy

    _____

insist again
on speaking French to him
as patchouli seance

    _____

anges purs the
"e" not quite
sustained but
anges radieux
ang__es__ radieux
the "es" extended
becomes a home
for your punished
wandering impulses

    _____

grandfather
gave me a blank
bound leather book
I began to use
as scrapbook, unfinished

————————

use his
maudlin watery
oeuvre as phantom
inverted-cock receptacle
like converting a foreskin
into shot-glass chalice

————————

laud becomes an object
to hold like a gold
Oscar-lingam
(Streisand's) forever—
on a clear day
you can see
Walter Benjamin
taking a bath

#7

[floral capabilities shut down]

Star of David in
chest hair asleep
on downtown F train

————————

thirty devices to "colonize"
I inappropriately said

————————

realism hurts Eric
realism interrupts Eric
realism saddens
Eric's mother

————————

Harrison Ford
provokes laughter
twice, a book of
Harrison spanking
literary cliquishness

————————

mi-
sogynist means exactly
what it says in
egg-timer fedora—
John Chamberlain's
auto sculptures
deplore misandry

————————

melopoeia
smokes weed
ash of Peggy Lee's
cigarette—beg
clemency from Peggy
Lee's cigarette

————————

exiled
from lucidity—
haecceity-kiss of
differently minded
Molly Bloom loving
red-bearded cousin—take

off your shirt, Jew
I saw asleep on F
train, velour socks

_____

       start to wonder
who the third guy is
and why they share
a toilet at NYU

_____

I pay for fried
eggs on bread like
expressive hemiola

_____

save cough for
doctor, don't cough
until I enter doc's
office because he
acts as if my cough
were a fiction

_____

Hillary's purported
secretiveness

————————

he called my
paintings decadent
shuttlecocks

————————

Apollonian profile
I tell him, triple
Gladys, Gladys is
triple Apollonian
shamanist

————————

    invent
new obscene Romeo
and Juliet miniature
poesy

————————

    begin
counting syllables again

to achieve modicum
of forethought—
counting circumvents
self-consciousness—
let five be magic
number to hear thrum
one by one by one

_____

Brad at my dream's
table said something
possibly offensive about
presence of two Brads—
earlier Brad was
unkind Brad,
second Brad was
generous Brad
wearing silver
Batgirl costume

_____

each poet had a duplicate—
I could say a catty
thing about the offensive

male poet without harming
the inoffensive male duplicate
also sitting at the table

———————

after Beethoven
specialist's recital
I didn't go backstage
to congratulate him

———————

bleached
faux-mohawk
desires abstinence

———————

active hips
smelling of a just
finished cigarette

———————

I changed
mentally to *cognitively*—

cognition a charged
code word

————

Jabès wrote
Book of Questions
on the Métro

————

floral capabilities
shut down

————

cygne-mot
cygne-monde
Sigmund

————

gay decoder
unravels
Nazi doublespeak

————

gay decoder
killed for
code-sapience

_____

modern communication
and proprioception
founded on
sacrificed remains
of martyred gay
decoder of Nazi
doublespeak

_____

= untangle,
please, our
unconscious
always-already
Turing-marked
mental apparatus

_____

time now to take
Brecht's full measure

————————

"it would have
been politic for
a Jewish nose
to disappear"
perhaps Freud mused
when the Wolf
Man said his snout
was vanishing

————————

my father's mother showed him
a newspaper article
saying Jews had lost
German citizenship

————————

forced to move out
of Berlin neighborhood

————————

"no opportunity
for emotional problems
at home—we had
Hitler to deal with"

_____

jewelry brought to police
department—swastika
outside door

_____

    his father came
home one day and said
"we're going to Caracas"

_____

ship nearly turned
back to Germany

_____

in Caracas they adopted
a refugee kid, who later
ran away

_____

    his mother
hurt because Gentile
neighbors in Caracas
wouldn't be seen with her

_____

64

after the war, neighbors
apologized—"What would
the German community
have thought of us?"

_____

already dead from
what we call
melodramatically
a migration-
broken heart
she didn't hear
the apology

#8

[pumpkin childbirth]

scholar inflamed water
with anachronistic
cannabis drops

————

      inserted my hands
under bisexual shirt and said
do you object and he
said he liked it—but didn't
reciprocate by reaching under mine

————

      desire
intensified by talking
to my father two nights
ago, 87th birthday

————

      lifeguard
said he'd marry me

_____

with scarlet pants, maître d'
hairy wrists, scarlet
pants, Lacoste
white cardigan, and beads
looked like a spanked legend

_____

      my voice
already ruined and therefore
incapable of being further ruined

_____

singing impromptu plaint
about a pregnant Pierrot

_____

we played the mimicry
game in a witchcraft
Birne territory like bourne
or burn bitterly in search
of somatic similarity

_____

railroad guy reading Philip Roth
didn't return my stare

———————

        write 900 pages
about a dead gay man, bloated
book about premature demise

———————

she who introduced me
to "Getting to Know You"
is dead—Mrs. Leaf
best teacher hosiery's
dark vertical seams

———————

capture beer can's
reflected green glow
on white paper bag

———————

glow on 19th-century grand-
father body, booby-trap
breasts insignia-tenterhooks

———————

shame derailed
my fourth-grade *Nudism Handbook*

———————

close eyes
and fantasize about erasure,
retreat, summation

———————

or dogwood tree
dog-penis blossoms

———————

shitting a pumpkin is childbirth
says Shulamith

———————

Grieg
borrowed flashy effects
from Lizst, jumping between
keyboard's low and high climes

———————

eat nautical-themed
polenta vegetarian
flan shaped like eel
while wearing teal
or lavender slacks

———————

Hammond Street house
where my newlywed parents lived—
buxom skinny
pale mother standing
on circular porch balcony's Titanic

———————

group of boys
overheard on 23rd—
"want to know what city
I never want to visit?
Paris—it's really gay"

———————

      I *arrogate*
said Emerson—Karinne
calls herself the "scholar-fairy"

———————

Ciardi my mother's freshman
teacher translated Dante

_____

Sebastian Venable's
summer poem recited
by Gladys Kravitz, nosy
Bewitched neighbor

_____

pee landing or leaching onto *King
and I* underpants, long line
Gertrude Lawrence oft-
circulated something wonderful
ululation of "Getting to Know
You" incommunicado

_____

      Françoise Dorléac
is "warmer" than Deneuve
says trustworthy J. Hoberman
in taxi after Jewish
Museum panel discussion
about Jewish TV

although I no longer
watch TV whether
Jewish or not

_____

when the pustule
vanishes, a pock remains

#9

[more kink per square inch please]

stumbling
cautious skinny elite boys
abandoning mentally ill fathers

———————

the minim method
of Seurat or Pascal

———————

Big and Tall
shop, no tailor will handle him

———————

steal her stuffed animal,
zipper instead of a mouth—Cesare
Lombroso criminology mouth-zipper

———————

Virgin Queen Bette Davis
bald wig and pleated ruff

in St. Croix suntanning
like violet-eyed "salty-mouthed" Liz
drinking Jack and Cokes at Sardi's
after *Little Foxes*

_____

changing your mind
about Wordsworth's change of mind

_____

protectorate
Barbra fishing for WWI
causation—whose guns,
whose gimcrack?

_____

infected taupe birch
remedies cut abstraction

_____

soma-a-tude—
Soma's attitude, if a
somatic vision got arrogant
and father-criticized

—————

father tells Soma
"you're arrogant and passive-
aggressive"—who is Soma?
Disney's *Hemo the Magnificent*?

—————

bearded father has negligible
chin I notice while he sleeps
with crayoning daughter on his lap

—————

pay attention to Berlin's
exit, *aus*, detrain
now, *aus* ass—is *Ausländer*
also outland ass? into ass we
out our portion?

—————

push-up is ice cream
treat and seduction tool

—————

stranger's car door
opening in folklore,
Reader's Digest warnings
about porn rings

———————

Max in Ibiza on Tony Duvert
binge, fashion train bling
Duverting him toward ingot—
why ingot? in *Gott* we trust?

———————

      train passes
near my former home
I presume still
exists—porch and columns,
lunette, remorse *dimanche*

———————

cut finger blood
bright Kandinsky
word-sun sun-king
wearing Vera scarf

———————

playing sexual Marco
Polo in swimming pool—
concussion high-dive

————————

Martha
Stewart's lesser white purse
is Frank Loesser

————————

her shoe limes—temerity
to say "shoe lime," accidental

————————

should I ask what and why are blue
diapers everywhere in his house?

————————

Deutschland über alles,
Der Freischütz hunting me—
occult Caspar David Friedrich ghost town
repeating "awe" for forward
motion in deracinating aria

————————

Beethoven in
Heiligenstadt mercy-killing childhood

———————

the youngster razor-blade apple-bobbing—
Tootsie Roll Halloween paranoia

———————

darkness Koestler
forgetting Lucille Ball's *Stone Pillow*—
did Liz ever play
a homeless water creature?

———————

we loved Mussolini's
flush toilets in Modena

———————

Vivienne Eliot in fourth
grade peeling carrots—
insanity "kitted up"
in mackintosh

———————

I'm impressed, my father
knew Liv Ullmann and Bibi Andersson

—————

I'd marry Cary Grant if I were Dyan
Cannon but I'm not Dyan Cannon

—————

is Rose Leaf, my first-grade teacher,
the origin of impetigo? can
you get impetigo under your eyelids?

—————

a smarmy jam is smarmalade
or smarmite, Marmite +
il faut que j'aille cherchez
un livre = rabbity Marmite

—————

non-girlish Vivienne's curved steeple
a Mama-undermining titmouse—
but cross out "titmouse," forbid
uninterrogated mood-painting

—————

it's possible to be a "terrible two"
when you are 56

———————

more kink per square inch please

———————

      do I have a queer
ethic? yes I have a queer ethic—

———————

queer ethical forsythia
uncolonized lesbian
sisters reading *Martha Stewart
Living* in Darien

———————

      slow-voiced masseur
object-relations Toussaint L'Ouverture
stamp-a-holic

———————

nebbishy Daryl Hannah doll
gap in space between dial-back

John-John and death row criminal
exoneration DSL or YSL—

—————

liberated rocks between rotted
wooden train trestles

—————

Felix arising, Felix culpa?
chatterbox tattoo

—————

imagine wife's orgasm—
his parsnip parsimoniousness,
blunt-fingered

—————

anyone who
mispronounces *frisson* had better
not lord it over me in any other
departments

—————

"oral sex! dope
ass!" writ on corrugated metal barn

_____

I like your blue door I'm
not sure I like my blue
door maybe it needs to be green

_____

my Marxism is
soupkitchen songful
Warhol volunteering

_____

are those her breasts on his iPhone?
is he writing a sexual message?
can I enter
his message as in *Minority
Report* starring Tom Cruise?
would it be fun to sext an angelic
hipster with orange rainboots,
belly hair, purple Polo slacks,
beer breath, and a start-up fortune?

_____

I'm in the presence
of male responsiveness even if he'd
earlier declared himself male

ergo unresponsive, cruelly unwriting
my body by refusing to answer it

_____

"want some nuts?"
I'll suggestively ask him, "but don't
put your fingers in the nut pouch
unless you wash your hands first"

_____

red lipstick on her teeth
as she encounters his big orange
painting, Childe Hassam shirtless
like Thomas Eakins

_____

admit that we find Childe
Hassam's body attractive, ungroomed,
scarred—if *plenum*
means auxiliary senses
beyond touch and sight
and the other pedestrian standbys

_____

maybe ultramarine is again the solution,
ultramarine as base and superstructure,
return and embarkation

_____

why did I turn
my back on stalwart ultramarine's
obscuring yet consoling ground?

_____

an ether sky pretending
to be sightlessness
penetrable by points
and lines if painstakingly
and casually the pitchfork strikes

_____

good not to have
sequestered myself in devotion
to ultramarine despite
its call to my worse
or better nature, if humans have
natures rather than notations

#10

[Clytemnestra's schnapps]

dreamt wallet
fell in toilet

_____

Nepal earthquake

_____

yellow-orange daffodils
in blue vase auto-
immunity scholar gave
us 20 years ago

_____

don't ask voice
teacher for permission, just
touch my nose while I sing

_____

explaining Sprechstimme
to the man on the moon

––––––––––

dreamt Mrs. T. peed
on floor, or did she sit
neglected on a towel?

––––––––––

he'll remove wax
chunks from my blocked ears

––––––––––

                girl cries
and says I'm tired, I'm
depressed, and then says
nothing more

––––––––––

could have bragged my
father knew Angela Davis
but did he really know her?

––––––––––

why did Anna Moffo get
a nose job? did it
alter her resonance?
how long a convalescence?

_____

"stuffed ears" sounds like a dish
at a cosmopolitan restaurant—
ears *farci*

_____

repose was gift I
spurned, most words from him
I feared because
they were triangulated

_____

　　　lemons
match and augment daffodils

_____

Speaking Ill of the Dead
is another book idea

_____

Huppa-huppa ride-a—
to explain what that enigmatic
sung phrase meant, write
a disquisition on *Tante*

----

no funeral for Aunt Alice
who witnessed domestic wreckage
and mother-knife

----

dreamt last night
she rose from the dead
and stabbed father
in the eye

----

did Sontag
read "The Law of Genre"?

----

find the photo of Claude Cahun
posing as my refugee
neighbor auditioning for *Carousel*

Peter
Hujar's lover called me a sissy
intellectual, a dying breed

———————

blue irresolute used condom
on hillside for Verdi
baritones climbing almost
as high as tenors

———————

a Sophia Loren
Sachertorte movie

———————

a hobbyist whose full-time
job is pretending she's friends
with celebrities—Mariah
Carey, Queen Latifah,
Bradley Cooper—more
about Bradley Cooper please

———————

dreamt loose cum dripped
or spattered all over my
chest and belly, maybe
three times as much cum
as customary

_____

       drooling
in red tulle gown
and succumbing
to compulsive cough
like Dora's famous catarrh

_____

video of guy who comes
without touching his cock
while doing pushups—
video (frightening)
of guy sucking himself
sitting in a rocking chair

_____

       riding Tante Alice's
lap on rocking chair—
"ride-a" might have been
Reiter, rider

_____

find *Shulie,* Elisabeth Subrin film
recreating Shulamith Firestone

—————

           smell
burnt wet arson house,
look inside and see
a stuffed Eastertime
animal amid ashes

—————

car crash, handsome son driving,
his mother almost killed—
I faint at sight of her swollen
contused head in hospital

—————

explain *Elektra* schnapps—
Clytemnestra drinking schnapps?
Orestes dispensing schnapps?
Chrysothemis pouring schnapps
in her own ears
to improve her hearing
or to approach Dionysian
origin of Elektra's primal thrust?

—————

to think and sing
Clytemnestra invents
invisible schnapps
viscous in a mouth
neutral enough to leave
unmodified the rancorous nectar

#11

[Popeye's teardrops]

bromance on toast with
side of sister potatoes—
conceptual restaurant,
psyche-as-luncheonette

————————

shamed to incarnate
dessert's death threads

————————

       Franz Wright
died yesterday

————————

Popeye's teardrops

————————

reading Michaux
aloud on subway

————————

my life's task,
self-elected, has been
to animate other people

———————

a book of lyrics—
call it *Kids, Please
Rescue Me from My Plinth
of Suffering*

———————

2016 Avenue N
corner of East 21st
#2D, apartment
where I was conceived—

———————

mother says
"note the prunes"

———————

ostrich or leopard
on his shoulder

———————

       send mother an eyeglass
repair kit and Wallace Stevens,
read aloud Edna
St. Vincent Millay's "Renascence"—
grow hypnotized by mother's
stories as if they alone advanced truth

_____

thick calves of tattooed man
holding ice cream cone—
find logic of his dark hair
and his exit

_____

       eating
a bookmark, using its edge
as razor

_____

       is *elusion*
in Thomas Hardy
a real word?

_____

to float the chicken
as hygiene pitter-patter
measuring God's fingernails

———————

he says bluntly "she gay-
bashed us" as joke, you
will find this offensive
because you Daddy are
a Roman Catholic comparison
shopper zipping up dinner

———————

cute musical-comedy tennies
tight-fitting gray hoodie
and quick walk because of
Guys and Dolls competence

———————

dreamt I was on a panel
with Hilton Als at Dia—
preponderance of cuties

———————

Leibniz mouth of all
possible mouths singing
Broadway

―――――――

        Stevens mentions a
woman's "horny feet"—
why are the woman's feet horny?

―――――――

she wrote fake books
about how to unclutter—
this book I'm writing
is also a fake book

―――――――

Pee-wee Herman
or that guy who specialized
in *schvitz*, steam, and squash
with his rabbinical students

―――――――

        rock star with V-
neck shirt and curly

fine hair and a beard not
groomed—first encounter
with beard near
a druggie's phonograph,
his LSD 45s I borrowed

————————

caption for new painting—
"He Became Discomfited"

————————

       Jane Marcus's
memorial

————————

Jane and I talked
about fancy purses
purchased on sale

————————

Ptolemy was Cleopatra's
gay brother?

————————

"too
many pussy willows
on this site"

_____

—any chance I
could see you before you
vanish into ether,
Johnny Weissmuller
smoking grass

_____

headache
from singing Schubert organ
grinder's lament

_____

I once knew
a woman who threw
her baby against a wall
and her ex-husband set
up a legal order forbidding
her from seeing the kid—
but then the kid

turned 18 and became
curious about the mother
who'd long ago thrown
him against a wall

———————

les lames
means blades

———————

I did a monologue
about Kate Moss's
emotional neutrality

———————

dreamt I told Aunt
Alice that Anne
Frank had an affair
with Heidegger and that
Anne Frank was
pregnant (with Heidegger's
child) when she went
to the concentration camp

———————

Alice fainted when she
heard this news—
the deliquescent style
of fainting, when she physically
disintegrates and reveals
(through fecal devolution)
that she is already dead

———————

in train reading Max
Jacob without looking up words
because I want
immersion in what I don't
know plus surreptitious
erotic contact

———————

bespectacled nude man in
boxed image surrounded
by inexplicable hieroglyphs

———————

      I compliment
the vein in his arm
and touch his demi-belly

    ————————

    turned down
offer to profile
Catherine Deneuve

    ————————

traffic in Weimar
across vegetable bridge

    ————————

many falsely aver
they are otters

    ————————

    enjoying
Monteverdi's bottom

    ————————

    take
off fuchsia sweater
so orange shirt will lift
up, exposing a belly
not worth exposing

    ————————

embarrassed
about unkempt father's
toothbrush in shirt pocket

_____

waiting for father
to notice that it was time
for me to start shaving—
he never noticed—I wanted
him to buy me a razor
and shaving cream and teach
me how to use them

_____

summer
only begins to come
alive when I discuss
clandestine filaments

_____

posing as an ingénue
when I am not an
ingénue and have never
been an ingénue—trying

to take a selfie that makes
me look like an ingénue
or at least like a beefy
Jewish novelist with
adequate erotic credibility—
a suburban Jewish novelist
with a stud track-record

———————

accidentally got
Fanchon red on my
finger and contaminated
the lunar parallelogram
with a red smear

———————

     why
did yesterday lack gusto
but today possess a minor
yeasty gusto?

———————

     video
was silent until he spurted

———————

when
he came anti-
climactically erupted
two long sighs

#12

[ode to recent air]

       mutual suck
in his townhouse
injudicious

————————

*The History
of Clean Faces*

————————

Stock Market Nudes

————————

Vuillard tearoom glue
distemper on canvas

————————

ode to
recent air—
it was

not my air and
I suffered as
a result, my
air ended and he
berated me
for air
ending
slowly and un-
fortuitously

————————

if I were to draw a
flower I would call
it *Ode to Recent Air*
and question the flower
for failing me—in need
of strong medicine is
the flower, accruing
significance upon its
wet shoe aghast,
a divergence in
orange or green,
a cast of Erinyes
or Aesop's fables and

inundation cold
and warm at once

————————

orange dress, do I
have a right to
record observations?
mother fell and hit
her head

————————

dreamt I ate brilliant
pink oil paint—
unsure if it was edible
I ate it anyway—
it tasted unpleasantly
metallic, like a spoon
or fork straight out of
the dishwasher

————————

keep your hand moving
for one whole minute
even if the motion seems obscene

————————

she punitively praises
the "made thing" over
spontaneous utterance

————————

high square
hair's youthfulness
dominates consciousness

————————

     buttock
creates new horizon
responsible for comprehensive-
ness but hair alone
holds sway, curl above
declivity—ask
questions of it?
don't embroider
its wall

————————

     others
use their faces as

fences and we take
their beauty literally
as a sign of remorse,
but beauty, an inter-
ference, won't yield

_____

dementia is cognition
smearing itself

_____

    we discussed
techniques to disguise
compromising sexual confessions

_____

    a handbook
of cheap wigs
purchased long ago at
the Alhambra or a music
shop in Seville
where they didn't carry
La Rondine piano-vocal score

_____

at Providence
café my sunglasses
almost flew into the
toilet—I rescued
them from drowning
before they got contaminated

_____

plaster wall's dent
and bedspread's curlicues
need to be described

_____

sizable calves, thickness
and roughness of
hair as it presents
itself to flat hand,
palm receiving hair
not as insult but as
greeted plateau

_____

our friend's
brother is a stack of rocks,

a ton of drying dying
butt-oriented Jackie Gleasons

———————

knowledge
forms around the word
or, a place for indecisions
to congregate

———————

your lava
produces lava in me—
I want to tell intemperate
vascular details,
a blazon of your
satyr characteristics
catalyzing flame,
combustion, and nutting—
call it snow

———————

narrating his cleft,
demanding close description

———————

listen to Gigli for diction lessons
and then vowel-declaim
"forcemeat, vein, noon, nun"

————————

symphonic condensation
of childish nipples
slides egoless
toward language

————————

sore throat from trying
to read Gogol's
Dead Souls paragraph aloud
on A below middle C

————————

      examine
perineum-horizon to see
if vistas add
up to the three-
wise-men kaleidoscope
I anticipate

————————

recorded a new song
about Jane Russell,
Lana Turner, my imaginary
role in a Douglas Sirk
film, and Arnold
Scaasi's pantsuit designed
for Streisand when she
won an Oscar—sung
to the tune of Albéniz
"Mallorca"

————

      ate cantaloupe
from John Ashbery
farm stand, finished
reading Philippe Claudel
Quartier in French, recorded
"Vittoria" and "Amarilli"
with uncertain
vocal production—

————

father's fatigued voice,
dry from excessive Sanka

#13

[lube up language for kitchenette]

dreamt in parents' bedroom
saw them have sex or
saw mother rise nude
or nightgowned on top of him

_____

fosse = ditch, pit, moat, trench,
gutter, grave, excavation

_____

fesses = buttocks

_____

faun fosse *fesses*—
confess *fesses* in
language's fosse

_____

hunger centered in my
pink organizer, and he under-
stands my organization's pink

_____

teach myself
his vestibule's increments

_____

traced a Tony
beefcake image
pilfered from video

_____

FAQ about his *fesses*—
squeeze rotundities

_____

dove back into Scylla
and Charybdis spiritual
throwaway coffee cake
wedding-soup bingo

_____

dreamt writer took off
shirt to reveal chest
scars, then took off skirt,
turned around, bent
over and aimed rump

at me—offering it?
smelling of sage

_____

if destruction isn't
known, seen, or recognized,
does destruction exist?

_____

        vociferously
brushing teeth in men's
room, like clockwork his hygiene—

_____

        dreamt heard rare
recording of Anna Moffo
singing *Tosca*—
complete opera,
live, Italy, late 1970s
background music in vitrine
or shopping mall

_____

to be windblown
by Shelley a bachelor
poet legislator

———————

lube up
language for kitchenette

———————

global
glottal boats itch and retch
in vetch
invece (instead)
vicino (near)

———————

The Five Obstructions

———————

dreamt intimacy with Liza
Minnelli, accidentally nude
in a one-woman show—
flashing her crotch's semi-
phallic clump, she

came into audience, sat
beside me—wanted flesh
contact, faulted me
for not following through
on the embrace, sent
me to Judy's room

———————

then Britten or Glass
(Hockney or Kitaj?)
wrote a score for Liza's
night, an intermittent medley
falling short of audibility

———————

                    poet
donated boxed set
of Saint-Saëns's *Thaïs*—
a nonexistent opera

———————

          I observed
scholar jogging or crawling
blindfolded nearly
nude up stairs

———

we huggéd in a dusty
professor's-house attic
clogged with dress forms

———

touch the wife's
zebra knee

———

a loom steals
her vision, a looming bee
Acropolis, a tad Sturtevant,
expecting Charlotte Brontë's
mom a hindrance to Hector
misogynist against
(or "agin") Agincourt of
meuble a Balzac failure
of nerve to continue rabies
prevention—tight stomach is
rabies symptom and I
feared lockjaw
because I sensed inexorably
tightening stomach at
Sabbath sundown

#14

[Homer the entrepreneur of mayonnaise]

tranquilized bachelors in paradise grotto
query my father's candy

————————

describe spanking in detail
as new hobby

————————

    give details
please of Picasso's homo-
sexual activities before *Guernica*

————————

    Brahms exercises
co-signed by his invisible
mother

————————

    a meatloaf she
said was better than a symbol

in a short story and he
wrote down her words
without loving them

———————

      I'm being very
Wanda Landowska—horned
ecstatic overly precise and alone
at Saint-Leu-la-Forêt
with lesbian companion

———————

Hope Emerson in *Caged,*
repeat, queer
green consistency to Hope Emerson
imagined but not seen—
or Rob Lowe, queer green
insistent nude star smiling
on behalf of literature

———————

"smash it" he said,
referring to literature's
thickheadedness

———————

    "I'm the queen
of jocks" he said before
leaping on the butcher's table

———————

encore Liza (in dream)
lies onstage and I see her strange
penis-esque lump which
means Liza "has" a penis or
pseudo-penis—at least onstage—

———————

later she leads me to Judy's
posthumous bedroom—smells
like a library or printing press

———————

    liquor or
medicine I seek in Liza's
white half-size fridge

———————

I am logopoeia and she is melopoiea
but I want to be

melopoeia—can't I be logopoeia
and melopoeia at the same time?

_____

      bless you,
handsome sneezer,
Leo Slezak singing
"In fernem Land"

_____

grandmother's 112th
birthday tomorrow

_____

the swimming instructor
who ignores me had a nose-
bleed in the locker room

_____

      I touched doctor's
groin once and then apologized
and he said why apologize?

_____

I devote
elegiac Rachmaninoff ballad
to Joyce Carol Oates's *Blonde,*
appropriate subject for a late
Romantic threnody

—————

she is proud
to run a temperature—
I am proud to have
a mother who runs
a temperature

—————

always querying
my father's candy, always
spitting out my father's candy

—————

do fathers come, like
jeans, in pop colors?

—————

mentioning Marilyn Monroe
addictively because I am
Homeric, a repeater
of patterned stories that alter
slightly with each iteration

———————

Homer the entrepreneur
of mayonnaise has storied
San Francisco sunset-briefs
auguring homo-argosy

———————

        his feel-good
Titian versus my
feel-bad Titian

———————

        do a writing
project based on sightreading
all the Beethoven
sonatas while delivering
monologues

———————

birthday boy mentioned
pube forest

_____

    dreamt brother was one
foot tall, a permanent
baby, the smallness
cute but worrisome—would
he be accepted by his peers?

_____

"thank you for your hostility"
I said to mother's friend Marge—
I meant "thank you
for your hospitality"

_____

    breeze moved
window shade, knocked
over jade plant

_____

    forgive
my persistent striving

and my perpetual
return to striving,
forgive my defection
from the time I wrote
the poem "Composition in
Blue" now conflated
with the story I wrote
about curly hair

————————

twin water-glass stains
on imbalanced coffee
table, rattling blinds

————————

obscenely bright
light distresses the page it rakes,
scars, scares, slakes

#15

[clairvoyant apple cake]

Jackie Collins died—
so did a type-font
designer whose two
daughters committed
suicide because of mental
illness

———————

Warhol's
Polaroids of Caroline
Kennedy hugging a
watermelon in Montauk

———————

to assemble
a life from fragments—
Racine line quoted
by Pagnol?

———————

       sent him "chlorine-
scented felicitations"

———————

       he examined
not my privates
but a universal Ur-cock,
mine a reasonable
facsimile—I hold the lease

———————

       start taking abstract
photos of details and still-life
tableaux—project
the photos and then confect
precise paintings based
on those proportions, even if
I eventually deviate

———————

       happy
birthday Sophia Loren you
are 81 years old, you converted
crushed geraniums to
lipstick when you were 14

————

A Special Day
Mastroianni playing gay,
under swimming-pool water
dick visible in *Penthouse*

————

        wrinkled uncle
arms of slack Cukor
directing Audrey as Eliza
Doolittle

————

        why
do I think the lady
across the street laughing
smoking through screen door
was named Lick for
whip (he licked me)
or oral sex or liquor?

————

weighed 121.5 this morning,
128.5 last night—

how did I lose seven pounds
overnight?

————————

C. K. Williams died

————————

     Jesse
James are you Jewish?

————————

venerate *le rêve,* Revere
Beach condoms strewn

————————

     Buonarroti
Buonarroti the great calf muscles
of Rose Kennedy

————————

    is sameness
ameliorative? do geometric
forms repeating in nature
increase the amount
of good in the universe?

————————

    stealing or utilizing
my own dormant melopoeia

————————

my grandfather's mustache
in Maya Deren's *At Land*

————————

    I mentioned
Phaedra and Dido—I wanted
to say Racine and *dis-je*
but didn't want pretentiously
to use him as platform
for foppish allusiveness

————————

    I can
imagine him saying "I don't
want rhetoric, I want you to
spend time with me"

————————

crudely limned nasturtium

————————

    Monica Vitti
in Antonioni's *L'Avventura*
I said was the epitome of
indifference

————————

    j'espère
Casper the friendly ghost
Jasper the friendly Johns

————————

sensation of brushfire mustache
bristles on anus

————————

    Mallarmé
rejoins the swish
usufruct contingent

————————

have Coriolanus will travel

————————

Parker Tyler plays a cameo
in *At Land*—I explained
Parker Tyler's significance

_____

             is Jesus
grout-conscious?

_____

syrup-coated microtone

_____

I stare at her opera-blue
striped blouse, rock stud in nose
Desdemona said
to this guy I like
those bushes

_____

        cantor
living in my ear

_____

silence in auditorium
when I said "fag"

————————

     evil overstated,
alive to evil I exaggerated
the *ill* in *evil,* the *El*
in *Elevated* train

————————

vileness inhabits
your tchotchke side—
sidereal tchotchke

————————

my sin is Caravaggio
night-knifing a loitering
carnation-man

————————

little sir, a plump
Napoleon giving head
to Dido—can Dido receive
head from Meatloaf or must
Meatloaf give head to Dido
in the form of repeatedly
thrusting artichokes?

————————

the problem was roses
as donated objects

———————

burping loudly enough
to distract the heroine
from hard-earned centrality

———————

drink to me with thy corduroy
welts—*Weltanschauung*
of a corduroy lover

———————

pleasant white piqué wimple—
spliced with Brazil the mind
released its hemiola

———————

     Baroness with shaved
pubic hair in Duchamp film—
clean-shaven orchestra wears
surgical whites to disinfect
the cantata

―――――

     my last
novel (*Sticky Fingers*)
was plagiarized

―――――

inability to communicate
my sexuality to any
vessel but the poem

―――――

jealous of Fanny Brice
because she can sing
through her nose

―――――

pink squares sit on clumsy
adipose bottom

―――――

underestimated power
of pink gouache consciousness

―――――

write Delphine Seyrig's
story as amphora
for plural spontaneous intimacies

_____

      I kissed the apple
cake because it was a clairvoyant
wise person-cake deserving
kiss-tribute

_____

to fail at one vocation
but to flower in accidental
other vocations—to slide
astride the siren

_____

to imagine my culpability
when I was in thrall
to her power as
a remembered
hefty quiddity—
or do we just say "heft-quiddity"?

_____

article about Venezuela
today, world's highest waterfall—
to treat that waterfall's height
as violated Judaica and to
love the violation's scansion
said William James slowly
after death when cough drops
replaced all other mortal pleasures
including daffodils when
I failed to turn right
(a transferential turn)
at the Loeb—the lobe,
lobo, wolf of Vegas in
bloodred moon observed
by pink-shod baby

————

don't make me leave house
to look at moon until it
stops being dirtbloodred

————

       continue
reading Beethoven

sonatas to prevent mental
decay

———————

visiting churches in London
he said and then New Haven
spires I didn't know existed he
said and the Hebrides where
To the Lighthouse takes place,
the Isle of Skye

———————

mother saw Molly Picon
and walked to Prospect
Park—"it was a humble zoo,"
she said, "nothing
compared to Central Park"

———————

"Fern had the grippe"

———————

her brother
saw Paul Robeson in *Othello*

———

pauses to eat
apple sausage or
to discuss eating
warmed remains

#16

[kindergarten emergency taproot tableaux]

talking to
mother about bladder
symptoms

———————

can't chew a raw carrot

———————

"calling her cute is
infantilizing"—mother
doesn't like the word *cute*—
"they'd better not call
me cute"— "I like
your repartee and your cynicism"
she says in elevator

———————

Veriano Luchetti, tenor,
born 1939, sang Don José
at the Met—I'd never heard
of Veriano Luchetti

———————

       kindergarten
emergency taproot tableaux

———————

       Schumann on board
a boat stubbornly exiled

———————

failure's "obvious
swerve" unnerves
the norm

———————

       I can see
nipples through his gray
jumper across the room

———————

bodily organs imitating each
other says Ferenczi

———————

to "take a lyric leak"
César Franck dreams
of shaggy totality

———————

blancmange explaining
frottage—my jacket
and yours, together rubbing

———————

pink whiplash berries
happy to be picked

———————

      dead John
Wayne posing as a closed-
casket Joan Crawford
isn't clear

———————

intrapsychic compulsive
masturbator bourgeois
orange opium eater

———————

knight's
refusal to queen a
pawn or acedia-pawn
a sedate queen—or
acedia-pause
is *misterioso* or
a retraced Vinteuil "little
phrase" banked by rooks

_____

what is a corbeil
a Courbet loaf like date
nut loaf or loafing
around stop-frame date

_____

returning to Tippi Hedren
hit by articulate bird,
embodied opium Tippi, or
missed Mae West
at 42 she done him
please don't get
"meta-" on me

_____

a rehearsal con-
sciousness isn't a captive
or contingent consciousness—
he said I invited
you to an orgy and I
asked detailed questions
about the orgy

———————

Huidobro
didn't squander
or ignore
word-hoard
language not fecal but
golden lava—
imagine word-flow as
air, light, don't
hinder or torment
syllable-rush

———————

dreamt last night
actor deposited
dangerous family

in our house, a cellophane
bag containing
upside-down baby—
alive, but how
could it breathe?

_____

she says "cattle car"
as if she weren't from Essen

_____

        put out
the bucket and receive
hamantaschen or
Taschen the pervert
books I went to high
school with

_____

what language does to you
is a tenebrous massage

_____

Mark Spitz nude mustache
when orgasms were high

apples, George Eliot's
translation of *The Life
of Jesus* and
Fassbinder (he said) is
too intellectual except
for *Maria Braun* because
she explodes at the end

———————

"Rosa Street, a little
cottage, red cotton
curtains—I sewed hems
and buttons—not
a spoiled camper"

———————

again "2016 Avenue N
Brooklyn 10 NY—Dewey 9—
seventh house from block's end"

———————

"cooking kippers
from a can"

———————

     writer
in dream collapsed,
lying splayed on floor
of New York Public Library

———————

a swallowed or inhaled
hot pepper flake scarred
my nasal passages

———————

     Mozart died
a thousand years younger
than wrinkled now my
face deceptively is in make-
up handheld piano
pentimento mirror

———————

     without
racing or impertinence
she called herself "Purple,"
a dimpled
gotcha (cha-cha) nickname

———————

       showering he wore
a Rolex watch—aimed
nozzle-spray at his
crotch, pulled back
swimming trunks to let
water aggressively
pour in—I wanted to say
"our idyll is about to end"
but feared the word
would alienate him
or I'd mispronounce it—
is *idyll* idle or id-
ill—diseased Id?

———————

       dreamt Queen
Elizabeth gave up the
crown so Prince Charles
could eat cheddar garlic fries

#17

[empathizing with charnel]

special butter asking
for incestuous attentions

_____

      dreamt a shoot-
out at school, Adrienne
Rich (alive again) cozying
up to me—afraid to stand
we huddled, hiding from gunmen,
radical knife-wielders
terrorizing the university—
better than lazing around—
who was in charge of torture?
couldn't bubble-wrap the terror

_____

Thanksgiving in Köln,
cruising incognito

_____

            twin
silver-haired zebra-clad ladies,
men at urinal without
divider, *getrunken* leg
nearness, man with hat—mistake
Herr herein
or *heiraten* for marrying,
and giblets for *gibt* or
her *guten Abend* Kirchner

————————

Klee's fool
ein fool? raise bilingual
child dock-wise, *doch-weiss*,
wise doctor undoctoring whiteness

————————

gamekeeper penis
bush halo dream

————————

gymnasium for old men,
short-haired woman Paula
Modersohn-Becker, the

Wladimir whose last name I
won't remember—sand on
Picasso and also knife-lines,
Messer Messe knife Mass if
you doubt Christ should
be pubescent and spanked by
Max Ernst, my grandfather
spanking pubescent Christ
with reddened popo—58
Robin Hood *Wasser* if
the guy named squirt
had a hand in it

———————

Jenny is Innisfree, is
langsam sold or slow lagoon,
or *arbeiten* and tan
and a work-voice hushed

———————

      cake hand
girdling your auspices

———————

Man Ray's photograms
suggest volume and
scissored lines—are
to shit and to scissor
the same?

————————

      Mimì in
white jacket or my name
mimed—is mimeo
a mime, as in Pierrot?

————————

compactness of men who
ask each other tanned questions,
one a younger protector as
David protects Jonathan
as Giuditta Pasta misremembers
Norma—she isn't the divine
Sarah, a good minnesinger

————————

      I take or
undertake a tragic desk-

journey—costumes *Zauber*,
a magic onesie johnny-gown—
over coffee is it nature
to be over nature a smashing
smashed sameness? zoo
sameness, zoo tranquility
shrinking your EST training,
clitter-clatter
or Faust capital
punishment field-marshal—
and he with V-neck
doesn't recognize gaze—
gas is Innisfree
Innsbruck *Buchhandlung*
book-handler, if you
handle a book or a
Handel book like Olivia
clattering heels, gray high
suede, women not ashamed
of eating cake

———————

    boudoir
arts foreseen by baby—to be

shy in my presence
as salve against vulgarity—
to keep kicking him as love
gesture, Lorelei *mein* lover
my lost loser or afterwards the
writer sank shrine mustache
handling amiss thunder,
Ewigkeit eternal ultimate
thunder, tan like dead
Mark, no voyeur—
almost forgot Mark's glasses,
vision going bad and I assumed
Mark was old, in fact he
was probably in his late
30s or early 40s

_____

     playing doctor with
Bubby Schicksal

_____

     international
kenning ban, to place a
ban on knowing or being
known

————————

    Schauspiel a showoff
trinket-handler, does he
handle karma or books?
atheism and a schwa
for sure-footed modified
vowels in ABBA, glue
wine, a beverage
of glue, mounting an appeal
against small glue Jews

————————

    is it good
Nacht is knock munch,
knock the porn film the
hired *genau* the genome
now appeared as a
Cabinet dauphin eating
ak-mak hard-bread, sternly
barking white-man Excalibur
apologizing—enough voice,
not enough voice, insufficient
dentition not stopping your
operator tactics—a Reich is

simply a penitent tee-
totaler—a pasta-eating
penitent tepee manu-
facturer in our wrong
camp Heine broke his
thumb and Goethe worked
as flesh or fish
or red pike—is pike ever
red and mournful? saying
a mild soft yes

———————

are you going to the red-
bar root-beer
nuclear reactor thank
you? he wore striped
pj bottoms in hotel lobby

———————

      imitating Disney
cocaine, honey-star *danke*,
dunking you a glockenspiel,
Daniel a bistro belatedness,
Danish laughing pot-stickers,
if *nein* isn't nine or *nyet*

———————

     minus *Schwester*
a Western *drei*-sister—
can she be a normal three-
sister, a sugar-sister? a
tzigane-sister coughing,
a chopped Kleenex

———————

my work is to avoid
repressive trains, other
Dreyfus-trial exactitudes,
a European so-so roll

———————

     finish shaking
the Snoopy widow riding
our argot—a seminary
copy-cat horizoning—
becoming gradually a Monday
horizon—*conosce*? Croatia
calling, a glug glug *Schnee*—
is snow a benediction,
enough said? sad porphyry
sufficiency, Rilke's selfishness,

ragtag European distress
remembering the woman
who saved our town
hall from daily bombing—
taking down language
a peg—is a peg down
or up when darkly
blessed? fake? is
charnel faked? empathizing
with charnel,
cabbage-emerging

————————

or bathing on the telly
shore, banging a floor,
violets, *Krieg*-violets,
four-point tasty *Krieg*-
violets laughing, cackling,
boon companion autumn
hybrid

————————

how many nuclear reactors
are near Charlemagne's

cathedral? destiny
charnel counteracting Chanel—
which Chanel? Peggy
Guggenheim's Chanel?
obvious victim Chanel?
at gunpoint Chanel?

_____

opera is glum, last
night shrinking opera-
violence gloomy *sterben* die
diet clash is The Clash
still performing Auschwitz
Chemnitz *-itz* a bad suffix,
not itchy, just the *-itz*
of horror—to visit
a town where they all died,
curious to see a list
of the hugging population

#18

[albumen a family possession]

transparent typewriter-key
lozenges advertise cocktails
in Köln

————————

testosterone's
novelty in his adolescent
system, mind stunted
or stunned

————————

dreamt S.
nude in my bungalow
but he was straight—
his anus winked at me
through a singlet thong,
an aperture of cloth,
leather, or fiber,
framing the anus and
making it easier to view

———

pretending the machine
is my mother, pretending
my mother is the machine

———

        confusion over
prose-as-tunnel,
loud smothered potsherd
voices rapping hard, and my
gradual ascent to invisibility

———

        sang along
with Richard
Tauber German
folk songs, wordless
hum, transposed
an octave downward

———

        finding
boundaries between adjacent
pockets of time
reprehensible

164

————

    a half
Band-Aid on wood
floor

————

dreamt Theater 80
St. Marks doyenne asked
me to write a paragraph
about her financial excellence

————

dreamt of Marianne
Moore ephemera
no one knew
she'd written—a conceptual
poem, an "is" next
to an "is"

————

    on the next page
a more keenly conceptual
poem, objects
stacked together
as if they were words

—————

someone pointed
out a photo-poem wherein
Moore had lined
up Rieslings in a wine store—
a Bacchic stanzaic
ideogram

—————

Moore had also written
a book-spine concept-poem—
a shelf of various books, spines
facing outward—amassed,
the words on the combined spines
composed a single poem

—————

at Theater 80 St. Marks
troops moved in Birnam-
Wood block formation
across the stage

—————

　　　Ligurian
village high on the asking

hills like a silent squirrel
or an intellectual
sleeping with a piano
Orange Julius—
a leak of faith

_____

can we learn how to enter
our own hypothesized albumen
photography?

_____

a mature partying lesbian
listens to the news and recreates
a father's BBC martyrdom

_____

"O Tannenbaum" initiated by Prince
Albert—Queen Victoria's
Jewish children

_____

did William Burroughs say
a writer's one obligation

is to transcribe
present-moment sensations?

_____

Thus the Happy Boy
Chose Crullers

_____

Gore
Vidal Is a Softie

_____

Percy Faith + Percy Shelley
+ Perry Como

_____

is his
belly flab parochial
or patriarchal honey shadowing
my own striving hand?

_____

coughing baby
Nachtigall handed the last

hankie to Joni Mitchell,
Kant mentioned in a
mumble—couldn't understand
his oral selfishness

———————

my head looked huge in the mirror
last night—because
my hair is long? how can we
discern psyche's lineaments?
can we gloze
psyche's handkerchief, can
we gloze the handkerchief
lineaments of psyche's habitat?
pretend psyche's ageist

———————

        you destroy (de-
pucelate? shoot?)
an English lad discovering
his mom's the queen
of sneakers

———————

start weeding tomorrow, but what
will I weed? how apportion
the caliphate?

————————

at the dinner party
worried that I'd
stigmatized myself
but excited by my cesspool
victory—the host's
cock, reflected in a shop
window, was a shared
family possession

#19

[Hegel's nose, or, hamantaschen *has four syllables]*

do you remember the earliest
plays? do you remember
the gods? do you need
to remember?

_____

       tell me a piece
of advice you accepted from Nietzsche
whether or not he intended to give it

_____

don't know what it means
to be German
or whether the statement
"I like Germans" is an obfuscation—
a doorway
to garrulousness and
linguistic feverishness

_____

take the word *hard*
out of my vocabulary

————————

thrive on cessation,
a new relationship
forged with punctuation's
hammerstrokes

————————

        rehear punctuation
as not the presence of
an event but its absence—
silence finally getting
a chance to be heard
for the loudmouth it
secretly wanted to be

————————

extend syntax,
shove it into shadow

————————

neurological
has five syllables,

hamantaschen
has four syllables,
obviate has
three, *justice* two

————————

Virgin Mary's
lesbian untouchability
as transcendental
signifier ("La Belle
Dame sans Merci") or
the Vicki dilemma—
whose words
are these?

————————

"Jabès isn't Jewish"
said Derrida—Max Jacob
tore up Jabès's manuscript

————————

thinking of Artaud,
Jabès said "the only thing
that interests me in writing"
is "the risk taken by the writer"

_____

Billy Budd's
mystical stutter

_____

imagine Fanon or
Meret Oppenheim
surviving psychotherapy
in Bulgaria hotel

_____

Martial's joke about Jewish men
being too excited at the bathhouse

_____

how few words can I use
and how widely and frequently
can I smile

_____

expiate
Hegel's nose
"uncounted experience"
henceforth I will be silent

_____

          forcing
the grown-up to eat baby food

_____

lead by example
not by stated precept—
make an ink mark to mimic
a childhood injury

_____

          the zither
but also the hand playing
the zither, and the eye
peering through zither-strings
to detect hidden patterns

#20

[the unguent list]

      throw myself in
ample handfuls of existence
in a direction where my body
won't be harmed or intimidated

—————

      time to remember
how slowly a father moves
when speaking
German, how slowly
a father moves in his pursuit
of what was wrong in
the earlier passage

—————

not wishing to be a
Benjaminian father, not
caring if bearded guys think
I'm intolerably flaky, not
caring if "ample

handfuls" sounds jejune
or phallic or sentimental—
do I want ice
cream in Marseille?

————

        I love
"sissified"—one could point
out the Plath
resonance but why bother

————

      lines are playpens
or measuring cups—if you
don't have a measuring cup
how can you live?

————

a list of words
that carry an extra charge—
call it the unguent list

————

intonation more
important than actual words

_____

what did witches feel
as they were led
to the pyre?
can I tell you
about the first time I heard
the word *quintessence*?
and then John Cage appears

_____

centrality of dance to all
20th-century aesthetic discoveries—
pleasure of lying on a rock—
soft sand versus hard sand,
Bergman's *Seventh Seal*

_____

write a story about a woman
walking through a field,
the end of the world

_____

choose an avatar, male or
female, and imagine that person
undergoing an unpopulated
adventure on cattle prairies

———————

insert myself in erotic
triangles from 1930 or 1940,
Monroe Wheeler, George
Platt Lynes, Glenway Wescott—
if I'd gone to Black
Mountain College

———————

and why have I
traveled so far away from
Maya Deren?

———————

Screen Test is my mother
because I test her patience and she
closes the screen door hard

———————

Screen Test is my father
because he grills hot dogs
outside the screened porch

———————

Screen Test is my older
brother because he got
a C on his geometry test

_____

Screen Test is my sister
because she screams "Reena" in homage
to the lady across the street

_____

Screen Test is my stomach
because Telemachus
is sitting on it

_____

mothlight is when I
slam the screen door and
Stan Brakhage hits me
with a bowling ball

_____

choose one part of speech
(conjunction, preposition)
and describe your relation to it

————

Didion worried
about gums?
stars must study
their own gums

————

purple is a good
onanist
cut to a certain thickness

————

the artifact's perfection is residue
or shadow of a fascistic
cruel procedure

————

he fails to express and so he
talks about expressionism

————

four miles from home
a cannibal killed, cooked,
and ate a thousand
people—recipes?

———————

families eating themselves—
alive rugby team
eating each other

———————

rendering homage
to Rubbermaid
toilet plungers

———————

trashcan feels empathy

———————

Dresden firestorm
blew out windows—
dwellers died in cellars

———————

authoritarians claim
no is yes

———————

acid yellow is the color
of suicide

————————

does Artaud ask Falconetti
"will you take confession?"

————————

rewrite an H.D. poem
using new vocabulary
or replacing certain words

————————

enter witchcraft's
tunnel and write
down any word that puzzles
you or provokes a strong
reaction of delight or distress

#21

[disgusted by my fingertips]

        father breathes
when I touch his back—brother
is St. John the Baptist—
mother took a child
psychology course

———————

didn't buy Sophia Loren biography—
gorged on floating island

———————

father studied music at Berkeley
with Ernest Bloch and Roger Sessions—
wrote twelve-tone composition

———————

Beethoven's Seventh
Symphony played at half
speed my father said

———————

Leonard Bernstein's
nose the gay lead in cosmic
upheaval or Creeley's essays

————————

"Toothpick" was
Sophia Loren's nickname—
Richard Burton's chest hair

————————

nightmare devil
bread, *Teufelbrot*
touching father-neck

————————

fresh slab
of Leonardo da Vinci
man fanning himself
with a newspaper

————————

wedding ring on right
hand is kitsch

————————

to rent in German
is *ge-rent*? pretend *gebruckner*
is to Bruckner to Bloch to
romanticize albumen arc

———————

      does shame
show up as fever?
two-bit beech tree a glossary
of Beach Boys if they
pull down their shorts

———————

      I saw
a Kennedy nipple
imitate a clam in slow
wet movements or babyish
guzzling in a cup, wiping
dahlia mouth

———————

Alex Israel on a magazine
cover—paella in our *Tagebuch*—
our daybook accommodates
paella

———————

write down the bathroom, dig
into the shame nugget

———————

disgusted by my fingertips
maybe means disgusted
by what I'm touching

———————

     I can hear your
sentences go click-click
to avoid panic
when the unanticipated
door opens

———————

     dandelion
nightgown with long
sleeves—I want to make
sure I'm covered up she
says, I want to respect
my own privacy

———————

          she is a voyeur
of your failure, he
is a failure of my voyeur,
he is a voyeur of my
inability

————————

women carrying ziplock freezer
bags containing classified
medicine, eyedroppers

————————

            a girl named
Jessie I held hands with,
and the next day she ignored
me, ignored the fact that we'd
held hands the day before

————————

        I volunteer to
suck my biology teacher—
he, too, watches my failure
and comments on it—
within my failure

I watch his observation
and diagnose its style

———————

bring the sock into bed
but what happens
to the sock afterward?
can you wear a sock
that once served as cum
repository, like the Dallas
book depository where
Oswald hid?

———————

　　　　Rose Kennedy
lived to be 104,
father proudly said, taking
credit for her longevity—
also he took credit for Angela
Merkel on the cover of *Time*
magazine, person of the year
facing refugee
problems, article

189

he can't read because he
has macular degeneration

———

      Caroline in
the matzoh box found
keys to a BMW, her mother
Jackie drives the emergency
vehicle I sing about

———

glut the darning needle's
longing, a longueur Garbo,
a Tantalus Garbo

———

as if Charlotte Rampling,
evicted from chronology,
had starred in *Camille*—
to be evicted by my mother
from my own carnal body
and to see depicted
the body I got evicted from

———

1920 my grandmother came
of age and voted, a newly
enfranchised generation of women—
for whom did she cast her first vote
and were her ears pierced?

#22

[lemon with vertigo]

       mother says she
didn't know she was
wearing lavender beads,
she wants to wear burgundy
beads instead

———————

       teacher carefully
marked my stories for point-
of-view inconsistencies

———————

my curly hair the origin
of involuted thinking

———————

       if Preston
Sturges *Lady Eve*
Lady Vanishes Hitchcock
Eve vanished and I took
her place or failed

192

_____

      she said "I could
care less about the drought"

_____

I stared at S.'s scar
so she nervously raised
her sweater to hide the mark—
did her husband
burn her flesh on Boxing Day?

_____

disgusted by my own addiction
to forward motion as antidote
to stasis—anti-Solomonic
pattering avoidance, moving
forward to avoid torment
of standing still

_____

      his mouth
gets amused and severe
when I commit a faux pas

_____

butt proxy—use
my butt or his butt as proxy
for what unacceptable desire?

————————

Schumann's doctor
reports in the asylum,
"on his walk he
often looks for violets"

————————

chartreuse
glyph sticky
on hand's right corner
keeps moving, gets
urban or pastoral

————————

is Delius jazzy? impetigo
or imagined red damaged
leaking areas near young
mouths—Carnegie Deli busboy's
irritated lips—Popsicle stick
wrongly wedged

between teeth for epileptic
convulsions

————————

google Elvis
at B.U., my father at B.U.
studying Husserl or Vedanta—
why not find his thesis
in a library?

————————

       she googles me and
discovers Smetana, discovers
genderless virgin, the place
we fought, grill
on Polk, brother an ally

————————

saw Debbie Harry in
big vehicle (license GROWNYE?)
exiting parking garage—
smiles wanly at me, pauses,
lets me claim the sidewalk—
and then I look back at her

————————

philosophy and technique
of bag gathering—
pick your least favorite
item and describe its flaws

————————

through the acupuncturist's
neutral needles, find the part
of your body driven to ask
self-impugning questions—find
the anatomical place where
manufacture of self-
castigating questions has
become a cottage industry

————————

even self-castigation can
be trusted, because it
has near at hand
a physical solution

————————

in the dark attic
they were shaming me

for not knowing how
to climb a ladder

————————

         crimson wallet
he gave me, a gesture
of contrition or apology—
useless, cramped, the billfold
Freud-signifies his ass—
but I ignored the object
and didn't feel attached—
shielding from my gaze
the object's inappropriateness

————————

         bodies
I hug and nominate
as kings of dream cave

————————

dreamt Aunt Alice
although dead is
momentarily alive again
and soiling herself repeatedly,

and I'm to blame
for her degradation—
she sees her own plight
and I catch her moment
of self-observation

───────

lemon with vertigo
never adequately addressed
by its audience—lemon
disinfects shamed drawers

───────

lemon in grandmother's pocketbook
or father's briefcase—
mother squeezes lemon,
throws it out the window

───────

choreographed
by the termination
aunt and niece are headed toward,
even though they appear,
in the photo, to be picnicking

———————

this photo will not receive
the glee I attribute to it

———————

teacher used Eau d'Hadrien
and I fabricated our aroma-twinship

———————

perfume bottle stored in porn
drawer—old dildos smell
like Play-Doh or the polyester
yellowed shirt I still wear

———————

give neutral attention
to unimportant objects—
ask a question
the object will
succinctly answer

#23

[conjugal eye-candy]

secured two good cruise-
glances on Ninth Avenue after voting

_____

    their father died and thus
pushy announcements and invitations
are issued—cannot death be
followed instead by silence
river girl pickle?

_____

    egg hash Avenue A
Temple Emanu-El department-store
wistfulness

_____

sneeze seize sees Nancarrow

_____

    fear of losing
grip on identity but wanting

identity to lemon-
loosen

————————

Dick Van
Dyke's Rose Marie yearning
for witchcraft

————————

orange
and green river's point of view
on John-Boy

————————

looking at
photos of Lee Radziwill online
last night after Hillary won

————————

qualify
as otter and then forfeit
your qualifications

————————

regain whale's point
of view—confronted
by simultaneity's
instruction book
I choose sigh

_____

sharks and jellyfish in Hudson,
I didn't put them there

_____

          brother quoting me
("battening") produces shame

_____

again the Cleopatra V,
land lying above
predella's broken diptych

_____

          smashed
flat face we know as sign
of vulnerability and want
to see destroyed

———————

Tante-steamed white rice
welcoming flush-faced
to apartment—Minute
Rice? flavorless, familiar—
limping grandmother
not mine—did they
speak German together?

———————

did he write the auto-
fellatio scene specifically
for me? smile, ardent
art-boy with pants gathering
at ankles

———————

guy with orange false
calf walking stern and quick
up staircase

———————

unfashionable
cryptic speech versus popular

cheerleading please-all
communicative speech—my
beef against communication—
it interrupts presentness

————————

miracle house on steep hill,
broken clay pots in yard—
nearness of house to river
stills consciousness if you
in the river-near house
are looking out—sun
on cracked pottery—
don't reassemble it—
enjoy glaze on fragments

————————

yellowish tarnished green
protects barn against
too much false attention—
identify with barn's
camouflage, where
mind's selvage
accidentally goes

———————

    concision suddenly
valued, and the smooth water
surface—decades of trying
to describe my sensations to others

———————

listening to *comment allez-vous*
and *très bien, merci, et toi?* for
basic comprehension and *chacun*
vient, chacun va and not understanding
correspondence between French
original and English translation

———————

seen by her children fucking
doggy style

———————

    like Marlo Thomas?
or anyone whose name on TV
I can remember, O. Henry
Teeny Duchamp?

———————

keep the puberty
shoe off-site—
37 dream
row boats wrecked

———————

say hi to Princess Grace's
ashes I announce on Avenue A

———————

repeat esemplastic
catafalque your mother
called and said I need
to see my children

———————

I cut hair
for the Shah of Iran,
I had an internationally
known hair salon on
Long Island, please
text me a photo of your
Vermont hot tub

———————

uphold arbor consciousness—
two young boys, shrieking in
shower, wanted to be warmly
towel-wrapped

————————

maybe Adrienne Rich
dyed her hair?

————————

putting labels on mailing-list
envelopes for death workshops, going
to his lecture, seeing mother see him—
father notices girlfriend flirting
with sailors at Durgin-Park—
fingering her in Buick
stationwagon backseat while father
and mother sit stony in front

————————

             wife sees me
cruise her husband—she guards
against his eye-candy fluidity—

maybe she studied
at school the arts of subduing
and controlling conjugal eye-candy

————————

"Mutter" was arty Nin-esque story
I wrote senior year, concision
blocking egress of material

————————

seeing Trump on TV
with sound turned off—
must fascist gesticulation
replace reasoned speech?
am I also guilty of fascist
gesticulation?

————————

     Ashbery postcard
the one piece of glory mail
I received on Block
Factory Road

————————

birds chirp but
what birds are they? and now
one small bird comes closer
to investigate

_____

my skin cancer
just a fact to bump against
like a beard's copper
patches or antique
correspondence belatedly
arriving

_____

loft bed shakes
when freight trucks pass

_____

he hated the sound
of a harpsichord
until I told him
its notes were plucked
not hammered

#24

[meat smell near museum]

LAX urinal stroker
retreats into stall—
I say no

—————

baby's maniacal cough

—————

Deneuve lives
in Saint-Sulpice coign

—————

   is Passover to
blame?

—————

it's Viagra's birthday

—————

Bette Midler's purple eyes—
Bertrand Russell's failure to

210

understand Cher—Descartes
in high shorts, hot pants—
Sonny, shorter than I,
wears confident shoes

—————

big black hat Gloria
Swanson up Bloomingdale's
escalator I saw

—————

gave aura readings while wearing
purple sunglasses

—————

       Spain Ronda 1491
the year before expulsion

—————

rock star likes
men not as cute as he,
lisp semiotics
shower eroticism I praised

—————

to demonstrate the sting
of being a desired object
she mocked fellatio to guy
who complimented her dress

———————

I love orzo I love bacon I
love euphemism

———————

Treblinka, Sigmund Freud's
murdered sisters, *I am the
sister of Sigmund Freud* and
then they gas her—

———————

trying to defend *fold* to
hostile room, cramming *fold*
down their throats, also *crease*,
narrow, *fundament*—does
fundament have a non-obscene
meaning? are buttocks
necessarily obscene?

———————

Pierrot le fou on an empty
stomach

_____

don't wait for six hours
and expect the six hours to elapse
without pain, Deanna Durbin

_____

why
treat human beings as vermin?

_____

tanning, I lay
in backyard, *Linda di Chamounix*
aria destroying consciousness—
must consciousness be fermented?

_____

supervisor
hated the sound of my clogs
on the bookstore floor

_____

my soil box can't exist
in the magazine containing
groin fat poem

_____

      clapping's
origin—when people
learned how to applaud
the book folded in on itself

_____

voom is room plus valley

_____

feared Gladys because
I thought her name
was Lettuce—
nothing wrong with the name
Gladys but it unnerved me

_____

      is Holofernes
a pop star dating Degas?
I said what art are you

excited about but he wasn't
excited about any art—
Diogenes is his Risorgimento name

_____

you can antique
or postmodernize anything

_____

overthorough description of brother
defacing my *Films and Career
of Judy Garland* book

_____

do I object
to the shaking or am I using
oscillation as aesthetic
constraint? Floyd liked me—
the liking red or green
in its legibility

_____

click sound in his throat from
mental illness despite handsomeness

———

tractor claw aloft,
barn blue, as if a truck
could be a barn's afterlife

———

Blake's shiny chest visible
in dark—emblem pecs

———

        pre-age the meat
by loving its questions, a zone
of meat smell near museum

———

cloven backside earns
Peyton Place mobility

———

write only when the words seem
an emergency or an absurdity

———

does my biopsy
photo qualify as the uncanny?
is silk-screening
too much of a drag? I don't
want to stray-bleach
someone else's dirty screen

—————

accept present
parties rather than mourn
absent parties

—————

find pleasure in action
and rumination, not in shop-
clicking, magical disaster
rivulets—in a raindrop
find your transient maker

—————

don't waste my life in echo-
chamber of laud-desiring

—————

217

describe why Tupperware
is metaphor—
hiatus in mind's
ability to function
without analogy

————

fat ass holding smell
kernels where grayness
beige brown copper
rust intersect and vitiate each other

————

    do we land here
where valuing stops?

————

    choosing
to think rather than masticate—
wondering about
his pickles and angularities, his
partner a dom or sub

————

to realize the pond
I won't jump in its slime—
to realize the brick
I ask Ektachrome colors
to declare their codes

#25

[all-seeing linguistic cruller]

did I say
uncles were always tragic?
did I say uncles were how
the infection of point-of-view
entered?

———————

not a verdigris
or bamboo
uncle or a showgirl
boozing uncle—eventfulness
dawns on him like jism—
but downpour confuses, *maman*

———————

the will to be
a druggie, to float on the
untethered nerve's vibration,
to approximate an all-seeing
linguistic cruller

—————

I want a nose hum—
qu'est-ce que c'est nose hum?

—————

being OK w/ omnivorousness—
smelly Gouda contents of his
belch-brassiere

—————

      being polite to your
own errors—enviability of the old
flame's three daughters

—————

untouchability, Weimar-like,
a texting basis for communion
Necco Wafers a symbol
for chalky fulfillment
and worthless stacked
parallelism and waxy
opaque paper coated
with sugar-dust—yet still
preferring Necco to all other candies

————————

a zeitgeist ruiner

————————

Tillie Olsen told me
"you look exactly like your mother"

————————

event horizon needing
Murphy bed to spring
from Harlow wall—roomie is Ida
Lupino not Joan Blondell
not Babette Deutsch's
book on poetic terms

————————

house had a square
pool but no pride, no sovereignty,
its love based on research—
drudgery Eden

————————

reprise motifs
to be symmetrical and ornery
and New-Critical *Axel's Castle*

222

————————

icebox geraniums—
"Dancing in
the Dark" the core of my
repertoire—*donc,*
he stinks of
acorn remover—concrete sentences
about Rome, *quoi*

————————

no longer tidbit management
or police evasion—
tumor a turn-off

————————

donut-eater
journal-keeper—
swamp smell becomes baby
simulacrum or tutti-frutti

————————

simpleton with nasal brogue
or nasal burn
in his Venusian

sinuses—grass so even-
keeled you kneel to kiss it,
grandpa

————————

Brahms exercises
as trampoline before dinner

————————

Xerox a phial
of Luminal, let Jean Rhys go
doubled into sphinx-sleep—
a prosody needn't announce itself
bossily

————————

to become one's own
mind's companion—not to dwell
inside the mind but to stand
near the mind as its
watcher, listener, confidante,
scribe—in the missionary
position we lie, subordinate
to our thrusting Yiddish mind—

224

why Yiddish? because my
mind (between thrusts) told
me it was Yiddish

———————

      —oy vey go home
swan's down
waterfall knuckle
sandwich is the napkin's
wet dream, *je crois*

———————

to be a crusader or nitpicker—
every crusade needs to bring
along a nitpicker—courgettes
and prismatic pristine
habitats—mother is the New
Jerusalem's crumbling
walls—if walls are singular
I wear your ruin
like a *voiture*
car-cousin—*voiture-voisine*—
neighbored by similitude—

———————

       and the hill's
demise, peppery
in autumn late I tried—

———————

       a photographic
error like a potentate's surrender—
momentary as a clam
or a calm family squatting

———————

his cleft dominates every image
tree I hang my pebble
ornaments on—but where's
his cleft and what's his cleft
to you or thee?
three clefts had he,
and I, no god
to memorize
the cleft's resurgence as a cow
or clod

———————

repeatedly inner Margit *ist gut*
is she a quid or Jew
oak mother

————

rice paper dragging its guitar—
loose Esther chiming in—
mother sang communist
work songs at hootenanny

————

not Ella my grandmother
private *espérance* if she
wishes to minister to the wound

————

why *dunque* why
sbaglio why *dov'è*
why Pasqua why libretto
why Io why Zeus
"bags of memory" staining
a Pasqua *Don Pasquale*
suddenly *sopra* Minerva
Giacomo Puccini

here is buried
Borromini and Carlo
Maderno and Jews
here are artichokes

_____

late the man with skirts
or soutanes *andare*
or *vorrei* as girl
inducement

_____

Meyer
lemon Billie Holiday
stream of *fanciulla* language
my beautiful red Salome
a jailer his Brooklyn jeweler
fondled

_____

brother in dream
gave mother a book with four
priests sitting down for solid
pizza *amore*—

228

I don't always wear it
out says the American
presumption of sparkling
leggiero—the priests enjoy
appetizers Moulin Rouge

_____

     shriek
of bird at 4 a.m.—
I thought the bird was a crazy
man shouting "fat lantern,
leave your native tongue"

_____

learning how to project
a factory is the slave
labor inherent to palazzi
and churches the row
of Tokyo Via Giulia

_____

     je veux
astonishingly red shorts
eye makeup

————

to stream the pink languages—
seek tomato one by one

————

"at least you never made
the mistake of having children"
father said

————

not Jewish gardens
of Caesar are *horti,* I stand
near his assassination site

————

   work
hard on your lemon
cathedral again

————

   the seen meal
the why seen meal
the scenic meal

————

if caste is important
narrative she sits on table
and complains about my pedagogy
finito though I beg
to be clement

————————

conjugality melons—
mother describes
having sex with father, expert
on his firm arousal—
semifreddo dad in
aperto open carriage elevator
Sunday *io* are
the kids fallow, is the
dong beneficial? why
goat or rival
Medusa's nose?

————————

Jew gym *guidicare* the
judged medicinal father—
Doctor Water,
I water the doctor

———————

if altar
be Kafka nose

———————

   gas mask unity O
tutti giorni the album leaves
falter, pay me to kiss you
in elevator but don't
force me to taste your ex-
perimental tongue

———————

foot, nose, and cleft chin
of Alexander the Great,
expressive thumb—
no peripheral vision
in fraternal lavatory
angers Dvořák

———————

   the 1926 Italian
government rewards Michel-
angelo and Raphael and Carlo

Maderno and Titian the
flagellated artificers

————————

      homeland
in paged brain, if she
dreams of the smoke
that is her husband—
brown fullness of factory
climes, *auf Wiedersehen
du temps passé*—

————————

      spliced is
how the light hits Cefalù,
not the scenic wayward
SPQR, steering Paleolithic
queers retrograde, institute
the forced Madonna glutton,
sugar the rolled sigh

————————

again the *Baum*, the questing
bomb, mezuzah *veramente*

spirochete, clamming up,
what was the hill, is sigh
matrimony, yes-festival *Inghilterra*
to claim lost tea
foreskin-whispered *parola*
the molten *langue*, crisp
sweater comparative Jewish
brindisi

———————

memory is king of humanity
no I will not
accommodate your capers
or your lederhosen,
mensch full of Skype

#26

*[narco-*La Bohème-*bacon]*

      glittering Jekyll
of Rimini fell
to the remaindered task, dreaming
up new maniacs for oboe and clarinet
and fossil, a trombone or sickle
trumpet, agitating cream
wafers

————

toilet sprezzatura and brio
the boy quotes me
as saying—punctual Ponchielli

————

      four braided masculine
chains—Sacramento sucks me

————

      when toilet frightens
she who called me darling

before I departed—a betrayer
departs for literary purposes

————————

       Pallas Athena Laura
Mars on Sunday sighting
a truculent tortoise
ridden by a baronial man
with tonsure webbing
his finite scalp—
ricotta staining
my ingress—pasted ice
is Midas, readied
obsessive carnivore,
unwritten vacation wimp-boy
fraternizing

————————

       a pure
David cherry is
populated by denizens
of attended miserliness

————————

     a quiet
should be sudden—
her lantern head-melon
a berry thanked

————————

     bye-bye
Babingtons tea room near
where Keats died, reserving
no water

————————

alert to Tintin to stet
to statins

————————

     probing
the machinations of strap-hanger
wives *La Wally* Rudy Vallée and
Alida Valli out for a cappuccino
hoping to make a cross-trainer's
Meryl Streep

————————

friend or servant
synching up with cat-fingered
psychiatrist reserving time
without people, yodeling

———————

Belvedere torso Ajax
contemplating suicide he
awaits Christian finality
stasera heartbreak *agace-*
agitation Laocoön a forged Rome
repeating *bellissima*
a thousand times my aunt's
orthopedic shoes—did my aunt go
to Italy? probably yes
to purchase a dulcet
Mona Lisa locket

———————

dream of madman narcissist
drug-abusing psychoanalyst
making pots or making taxi
wayfaring glottis

a possible swan, men in Italy
with *americano* beards not posing
forces the baby to eat

_____

pabulum gentlemen squeegeeing
signore's nutcase
brother platitudinous seas we
incarnadine the wretched
table setting
she assumes near Formica
blanche supper El Dorado

_____

    subito presto the
cello the harbor the petulant
number, my mother said
my brother but she meant
your brother, she meant
my son—a nine-to-five
duck platypus lost in *ondes*
waves

_____

ethnic return
of the screw, we borrow her
Paganini variations
lui or Luigi Nono
fermata, our resonance
exercise *insieme*
for the first time

_____

stomach
cancer at end of World War II—
should Stein not have been
allowed to escape concentration
camp in any way she
mustered from personality's
force? to deny Stein
the right (selah) to have
dodged the Nazis—patient
Celan firestorm instantiating
jaune Margaret or the
time I invoked Marguerite
of Faust or *Dame aux*
Camélias, thinking the name
Marguerite sufficient spell

_____

devil-may-care repertoire,
developing voice as intoxicant

_____

swell said by Harry in dream,
his legs alabaster Hermes
Apollo Belvedere misprision
a good Mignon factory death she
died in cigarette factory brawl
and we turned her death
into a chance escapade for
oboe again

_____

father gave me
credit for loving Chaplin,
I became the strange son
who loved Chaplin, no
good reason for loving Chaplin,
it was an *acte gratuit*,
unfettered, without
rules, according to no
one else's ceremonial decision

----

spit on lovers who came
late to Loren, who dithered
andante at gate—
Loren latecomers
leave because I ogle husband,
a Prince Hal Hamlet
deferring sovereignty

----

       smear together
two October heads for October
paste, *cotagna*, quince
Marxist mélange of
smeared-together bald heads
at chestnut dusk or blue *alba*
to liquefy their pediment

----

       or if I
prefer to be architect of my
pharynx, nasal cavity
I meant cathedral but
felt shame to repeat *cathedral*,

word I used to praise hyper-
bolically the dead woman

_____

          be attentive,
beloved eunuch *diavolo*

_____

in the mirror the eunuch
seeks not me

_____

Palazzo Altemps satyr
almost hard from
nearness of Daphnis

_____

thank you *al mare*,
the finite mother of
Largo Argentina smelling of
narco-*La Bohème*-bacon

_____

I do, I do, Ethel Merman
belted safely,
Pantheon an acoustic sculpture

————

"sock it to me" Judy Carne,
why did we bomb Iraq?
face of sleeping Erinys—
is he a sleeping Fury,
can Furies sleep, can Furies
be male? please gender
your ostracized Fury

————

      understand collations,
omnipotence on the found-wood
highway, my face
is burning, return
return O fallen soldier
but you are fallen
so can't honestly return

————

vocal Ludovico—
faun *fesses* I earned,
ass with strings

————————

regatta dreamflow
language and then quick
clamp down on *Dio* indexicality—
and so we return through *Dio* to
minimum boy indexicality—
proof of a masque bride

————————

Naples yellow wall
is dimpled, Caravaggio's
Dionysian boy-leg is dimpled,
thigh inviting us—
forwardness of Mannerist
nada destructive seduction

————————

aperture expands suddenly
a bambino works up
a shriek or banshee bark—

and I get tired like
Anjelica Huston at Ciro's
understanding Capucine's
mistake, a studious
bathhouse Athena

———————

pagliaccio-style
the one-eyed present-tense
stoned Cyclops knowing
teal endocrine Lent,
a cool German omelette,
informative and cunning

———————

orange lavatory
at the crematorium pisses
clean disadvantaged
cabinet of finite horrors

———————

the stinking
insecure smoking man with
untucked shirt and tattooed

gray-bearded serene
father—his dad is island time

———————

      change, say
the maladjusted cattle—no
way to reproduce this high
illegitimate commandeering
of my already controlled interior

———————

domenica punishment is Sunday
backwards hex über-coven
panforte jalousie interiority

———————

      Roman
shoes a simple band
of leather leaving ankle
uncovered—ribs sticking out,
juvenile braggart in
training pool *ancora*
ragazzi appetizing the earlier
ass grateful to be
operatically thanked

————

      syllables
crammed together—
how much Bernini-style
sculpture is devoted
to orgasm? Teresa
chained to orgasm
is caught
like Paul Celan by
arrested time—

————

      a tergo see
wife penetrated from behind,
son's point of view lesbian-sighting
mother penetrated *a tergo*
by *Mosè in Egitto* satyr-
father arrested by pseudo-
Bernini on path to orgasm,
the up-and-down servile
fish

————

      mascarpone like exculpated
Stein a gray-capped wave,

each word has a comprehensible
and an incomprehensible edge—
catch the place where a word
surrenders or crosses over

_____

voyaging (like a fish with
feathers) inside my human
head, economically
sirenic, mal-
adjusted, Keats tomb
obelisk present time thieving me
or I thieve present time

#27

[is the cookie a romantic nothingness rebus?]

in Bramante's cloister
consciousness folded

_____

mere exemplum *mère* exemplum

_____

excuse me for not feeling tropical
thick or indicated

_____

      prenatal fishing
trip *avant Sturm*
avant Drang
or is her music warring
with my music?

_____

mark a particular place
with boy urine not

boy wine I mean
carrion humanity

_____

private *allora carciofi*
generality mounting you,
flooding you with deprecation

_____

    we gathered
on the piazza with our new
Italian slapped friends

_____

    that summer
finding intelligence no harbor
we chose breakage because
Brakhage clarified our raging
or wasted intellect

_____

you find mirth in homoerotic
punished pockets,
the ameliorated Gentile
fosse

———

       guarding my
passementerie
Montale forgave his lyre's
impersonal music

———

at Borromini crypt
waiting for friend-words
that please me and avoiding
words that displease

———

imagine faun ass is
site of linguistic slide,
the quest for
the man (Gigli?) who
sings *maledetta*—
secure your curse, don't
let your curse float away
like Ophelia waiting
for the bank to open
or the journalist
to pity the flood's fumes

———

       when you
wore sneakers surreptitiously
and hurt your mother's feelings—
when no one offered your
mother a trip to Italy—

_____

what makes my body Sorrento?
or is mine a non-Sorrento body?

_____

when *oppure* signifies
ownership of the fork
in the road, sage-strewn,
to the maternal cross

_____

eccola the virgin's sameness,
how many virgins can you
fit on your bony simulation
of joke
conniptions? Cenci! cries
the phoenix, sick
of its incontinent ashen afterlife—

————

want to say "saved" before every
nominated object

————

starting to love the *Tante-*
skipped space and alert it
to bell tones of frigged
moonlight, the many
favorites of thought's
dubiety, dubbed film of a lost
fragola, fragmented strawberry
missing its supposedly male
larynx—

————

men here have 85 larynxes
like voice boxes in utero—
father and son are slammed
together and this book
lasts forever

————

mother's Parker
ballpoint in kitchen near
white wallphone

————————

said
"Ray Conniff" for no reason
near Ara Pacis altar
in Richard Meier skin

————————

Mussolini's name above
Teatro dell'Opera stage

————————

we call it
my pink organizer
and it bodes a new
sanglot species of the pause

————————

Heifetz Jesus never opening
his Rochester arms,
radio-free Jascha

quanto beve—a cougher's
intelligentsia coffers

————————

heretic
loving *Mandelbrot* salt
grain you beg for

————————

praying
to Tintoretto's closed
lines and using them
as butter guidance
toward the laity, where thrive
Veronese vagaries of
soap-bubble behavior

————————

she has six children, nine
or ten months apart, Wenceslas
Good King foolish king sad
to be turned into a song,
a believable ear infection à la carte
pomeriggio the shul
opens—dies in opening

———

eligible guys frequently
touch their own Tasso
stomachs in public

———

nudist champagne,
the dolorous "g"
interfering

———

Villa Farnesina—
Farnese folk decided
to miniaturize themselves
and become "-ina"-ish,
Parmigianino-ish

———

Caffè Lungara 1940
means Mussolini peed here

———

ciambelle al vino, in
wine you dip the cookie?

or is the cookie made of
wine? or is the cookie
a romantic nothingness rebus?

_____

      to dispute
the ungrammatical going-forth,
to Herzl-ize (make Herzl
candy of) the going-forth

_____

did Queen Christina love
her library and die
of excess bibliophilia?

_____

too broad, too almond-like
the centaur's lower half
destroys perspective

_____

"we are seven" said
the old man—he didn't say
"we are Swann"

———————

                      we lost
our documents and fled
into a shady or shed novel—
we shed or shat the novel
as we shat the viola da gamba

———————

I'll antique my orange remains
because I died young—
a death already past
and factual yet held
inside parentheses of going-forth—
we haven't hit death's bull's-eye

#28

[to grip challah, the arm Wiener-Schnitzels]

        holes in
his *parole*, when speech
is prison

―――――

        lick
Sardanapalus,
obey the best
swamp lest incorrigibility
of your own fluids sack you,
then explicate the sacking
in a daguerreotype

―――――

        the venerated
man with mustachios
is picking his teeth to float
thyself above
the phlegm *Reisepass*

———————

to grip
challah, *niente*,
j'essaie

———————

and then Serge finds
his own *parapluie*

———————

wheeling *leggiero*
a cream suitcase *soleil*

———————

men *niente*, can men *niente*,
C.'s penis in dream
a rude ballpoint

———————

sex with
son in Joyce-room,
room of chlorine-Joyce
if Joyce husbands her own
drowning—and the arm,
fatigued, Wiener-Schnitzels

———————

I pass all eroticism
through a fictional screen

———————

disponible Trakl

———————

        buy
her Minute-Rice teeth in
gallery menthol

———————

Dolce & Gabbana purse
small as Loge's fire-
brandisher

———————

your pale religious sister
with osteoporosis saddens
and predisposes me to *passé*
froid, go cold and past
into hebetude *vivre,* jolly
door into hebetude

———————

scramble
the *jamais*, upset the always,
tranquilize the never,
excuse the rotund—
I had a profound thought
about the rotund but then
I forgot it on the patio,
left it *cancellare* on
the *évidemment* the evidently
patio, evidently Cecil
you are a patio and
claim your patio-identity
as non-prosaic fief—
denuded without a *haut-*
Himmel injection of style
and smile

———————

by accident
I wrote an ellipse on my
hat, a *dîner* ritard
with turquoise beaded bracelet—
huitième chips on foehn

———————

malade baby trying out
its masquerade

_____

big-bellied financier
blowing the inaccessible

_____

       playing Rachmaninoff
in boozy fashion while
intoning "precipice-speak,"
a dialect spoken
by precipice dwellers

_____

reminisce about
his ass, a lost utopia
like Forest Hills, a gravesite
goat-fresh meadow

_____

careening Popsicles,
can we be our own cicerone?

_____

fat lip from novocaine drainage
includes Santi Giovanni e
Paolo in otherwise cubist
wife-compositions

———————

        more
water is the answer, more
and more water,
less Mattachine, less
machine-cubism, less Léger

———————

by-the-dozen modernism,
copy-zones, bits from each,
a line here, a line there,
insta-compositions, tease out
their logic—
lozenge thrills?

———————

        why not Alice
Neel upside down?
Sontag voyeur

with pink-edged
mirror on white table

———————

marmalade
—I must aid
my marred
mal ma—

———————

I must not mar
what ma has made

———————

I laid my ma
though she was *mal*

———————

I aid my ma
who, laid, I marred—
I married my marred ma

———————

     I rode
a pudding house—

not horse—
texte sans sens
or with freaked sense
like a flower freaked with pink

———————

      drumming
or thumb-pianoing
his schnooky groin
which I must not emulate

———————

Winslow Homer's pink triangle,
a Z name hump-festing it—
beef Stroganoff at
wedding's zenith, or scrambled
eggs dehydrated

———————

trying to reconceptualize
the void as an opportunity
for debauch

#29

[tuna music on a homemade tambourine]

      maze my
minotaur moves through
in two different mouths—
first mouth's owner
wears a hat

_____

my hat gives me
Noah's anonymity
without explaining
who Noah is

_____

      accidentally
rejected the redhead—
wanted to deviate
momentarily to include
the shy thick one
in the next booth

_____

like a chemistry teacher
who misplaces her Over-soul
or mistakes it for caviar

_____

can prosody be
safe sex?

_____

oral safety negating
his sunset cloud's rigged
fissure

_____

profile of trim laundry
boy with wedding ring
widdershins, octopus-like

_____

tithing it, her oral
circumcision ballet
reclining priestly
Ingres casualwear

_____

causal-wear, if con-
sequence is moiety
or motley Avon products
for dry skin perchance

—————

diction contains
class aspirations
writes Robert Glück
and I'm mister word
choice hence mister
class aspiration

—————

you presumptuous bride
of slow quietness
promoted by giddy
entelechy, my boss
Goody Entelechy
plastered in Paris

—————

"God" is simply
intention

—————

conceive life
as a series of intentions
rather than meaningless
accidents

————

I note my body—
that notation is an
intention—an extra,
it precedes and
stands outside
mere existence

————

to be grateful
for your toes is to
intend them and
not let them
languish unthanked

————

forego my
thee-ism

————

you had proms
I had glory holes

————————

to love formlessness
where land
gives place to ash

————————

can't help my addiction
to euphony
making tuna music
on a homemade tam-
bourine like a history
of the world stuffed
into a wine bottle
then corked and thrown
on the high seas

————————

giggling in a void
when I see short people
on TV, officious
toady creaming like

memory of Carole King
concert when she got
hoarse toward the end

———————

flattering Saturn or
considering a slatternly
approach to self-guided
astrological divination

———————

unlicensed petting in
the astrologer's mantic
office

———————

The Stigmas
of a Crocus

———————

did she bathe
with her grown son?

———————

German typewriter in
Lisbon with strings attached

———————

I returned to Lisbon
and found the theater
where the escapade began—
pink Teatro da Trindade

———————

the cinematic use
of butter—
BUtterfield 8
Butterflies are Free

———————

dreamt two babies
flew onto the Met
stage while Leonie
Rysanek sang Wagner—
flying babies bypassed
the ignorant conductor

———————

in the front row
I established eye contact
with Rysanek, who seemed
to understand novel uses
for the uninvited
aerial infants—buttresses
to uphold the martial score

#30

[abstract animal-crackers Crucifixion tidbits)

askew self-portrait
as *BUtterfield 8*

————

emergency clothes-buying
mission with her nearly
nude, martyred son

————

Sal Mineo in *The Bitter
Tears of Petra von Kant*

————

Gloria Grahame in *Tosca*

————

Sal Mineo in *Taxi zum Klo*

————

Roger Federer in *Fox and His Friends*

————

J.Crew was another
store I planned to
take the near-nude son
clothes-shopping

———————

splurging, I bought the boy
a red peacoat to assert
his presentability

———————

Roger Federer in *Querelle*

———————

Streisand and Tebaldi
with hot and cold
water spigots

———————

Renata Tebaldi in
On a Clear Day
You Can See Forever

———————

hot and cold water
spigots for Fernando Lamas,
Lana Turner's momentary beau

—————

Alice James—
"osculatory relaxations"
"parental bowels"

—————

Ramon Novarro in *Phèdre*

—————

Ramon Novarro in
Against Interpretation

—————

Fatty Arbuckle sings
"In-A-Gadda-Da-Vida"

—————

self-portrait as Renata
Tebaldi in a rain
puddle on West 24th Street

—————

self-portrait as Renata Tebaldi
in *Sorry, Wrong Number*

————

father gave me the Nuremberg
book—"scared
to death," he said,
"that was my childhood"

————

Monica Vitti contemplating
the labyrinth

————

"to scintillate your
way into the race"
I sing Monica Vitti
contemplating Saint
Monica contemplating
the labyrinth

————

Renata Tebaldi
and Roman Polanski in
The Roman Spring of Mrs. Stone

----

       topless Andre
Agassi amid animal
crackers

----

the pornographer has
principles, and I,
despite my ethical
father, do not

----

he ran a penthouse
operation for dwarves—
I was the prime dwarf—
with a folded male uterus
meant for cantaloupe
menses, Miss Fanny Tcherepnin
of the low-stakes piano factory

Samuel French
playwright stench as
neo-compensation for
uterus (mine) slowly

bragging, infinite—
to imitate Rilke,
careless oil crayon,
I want you, meta-
crayon, young talented
fox I approximate
Tenderloin grizzly bear's
ass-uterine projectile
post-Jungian fodder for
Satyricon experiments

—————

a red-stunned
arctic-blue somnolence I
can't predict or betray,
I can only steal *into*
the fissure, make
the fold a new home,
a crease I've been searching
for, hence my animal
crackers mode

—————

Sal Mineo looks cute
when running away
from snap judgments

————

stranger in
hot pants at the crossroads
is falling into a chromatic
abstract animal
crackers crack

————

I saw two
muscular, fearless birds fly—
yesterday I spied a bunny
on the lawn—the sunlight
(interstitial companion)
now clear and naked
between spurts of action

————

an active
hopping chipmunk, tail's
activity separate from

body's—front legs and
back legs independent

———————

Hitchcock
turned me
sideways
(thought bubble)

———————

read Simone
Weil for Crucifixion
tidbits

———————

     saw a sick
interior designer clutching
his khaki-clad crotch
on Fifth Avenue near
Madison Square Park's
"dog run" where
my friend spotted Jessica
Lange exercising her dog

———————

Candy Darling in
The Passion of Joan of Arc

———

underwear visible
through sheer tunic
the martyred near-nude
son made fun of the blazer
but then converted
mockery into advocacy

#31

[braggart deodorant]

diapered boy
in men's adult bathroom—
father trading masculinity
for kippers

_____

intelligentsia's
failure to breed
dandelions

_____

cultural wasteland
of not knowing or for-
getting to dwell
in the concentrated hall

_____

garbage's
expectationless knell

_____

ancient technologies
to sprint out of time

_____

to toady in past runnel-groove
Ethel Smyth or Pissarro

_____

aunt fell when the stranger snatched
her purse in the Richmond District

_____

      as if Ava
Gardner knew the inbox
where two technics interface

_____

"buttinsky" she called
the "me" person

_____

      remembering
the voice-break fossil, reaching
back to where voice cracks
or heeds its foment-fissure

———————

or the fossil who watches over us all

———————

I discover rain
boots beside tree

———————

      drunk Nedda
inexplicable rip in cosmos
toneless "Stridono lassù"

———————

in posthumous auditorium
I sing this *brindisi*

———————

clap me a riddle

———————

cult of ought
or aught—
afraid of canapés

———————

which means
braggart deodorant

————

      Charlotte Rampling in
Hush . . . Hush, Sweet Charlotte

————

diary of Alice James +
two guys I met in
elevator yesterday

————

the mystic jelly glasses
of Jean Rhys
believe this dahlia
is trying to make a phone call

————

sonic or acoustic tourism—
close your eyes in Paris and
are the sounds different
than if you were sitting
in a New York café?

————

David Antin died
yesterday

———————

seance pianism
to reclaim dispersed
or destroyed library

———————

was Benjamin correct
to say his briefcase
(or the manuscript
it held) is "more
important than I am"?

———————

Freddy Herko dancing
out a window

———————

pourquoi cette comédie
extrême de la
bonne fortune de ma vie
bizarre—O Dieu de

haut et bas et lourd—
de notre univers complet
et fou ou foule de grâce
comme le magique
esprit du monde outremer
vraiment espace de la
mort ou de l'amour

———————

in Cannes
Picasso drew landscape
incest dreams—
priapism night
maman street
écrit, a hand incest
behind the velvet
Playboy pillow
five Pasolini buttocks
Bataille librarian shadow

———————

Eléazar in
La Juive also a street
and sugar cookie

290

————

honeydew and
grapefruit, each properly
sectioned—dining
with senile aunt
who feigns competence

————

but every time I say
or write "my life" I perpetuate
the flaw

————

    uncorset association

————

word instigates echo
and I become connoisseur
of echoes

————

    can babies
say Mass?

————

distraction napkin

_____

green Kiefer
notebooks I never finished
reading

_____

czar and crazy are aligned—
craziest czarina—
the *c* and *z* create Jascha
Heifetz

_____

when Rubinstein
lifted high his hands
and brought them down to begin
the Chopin scherzo

_____

wish I'd been more loyal
to Jews—loyal enough to
learn Hebrew and, why not,
Yiddish—maybe learn
Spanish next year

———————

November 10th
Trump catastrophe
depression fear shock

———————

Mike's balls and
crème de menthe,
art in a damaged time

———————

dreamt of a fakir
or shaman—a tall,
plangent actor
with an extra
penis jutting out
from his right hip
like Alice Neel's painting of Joe
Gould with three penises

———————

this extra penis
(I recognized its shiny glans)
ineligible for patriarchy

————————

should a kind surgeon
have lopped off
the extra organ at birth
or did this supplemental
device give him psychic abilities?

————————

in the dream's sequel
the actor had no penis
at the front of his body—
just the irregular
penis protruding
from his hip—

————————

this transversal
afterthought, an organ
not sexual,
proved to be
a private aesthetic
thermometer—
a tool to detect
fever in the casserole

#32

[may we uncorpse the bubble]

dreamt someone criticized my
posture—said I craned
my head unattractively forward

—————

hat of the murdered
man—hat of the stymied—
swastika in a Brooklyn park—
statues laying
claim to nothingness

—————

made lines with two
green markers—one
marker was defunct—
I don't adequately
separate depleted and
functional markers

—————

the recalled
cedar lipstick she
wore—Giacometti
in sheer highchair nighties

————

Parisian debt cakes—
is Origen
the famous castrated guy?

————

eruption
belated as frizz-wall
against languid-paced Roman
nookie cherub
skeleton out-nostos out-
nostalgia, sick ache
neuralgia, sensualgia—
sick of the sensual father—
may our fourth finger
linger, may we be
caught dead lingering, may
we recapture Marsden Hartley

————

may we uncorpse the bubble?
mais oui, uncorpse the bubble

_____

being inwardly sodomized
by go-getters with one
rouge-blind eye

_____

     slowed
large mom *Juden-*
courageous at a processed
slant—rejected
cheese is a sedative

_____

red macaw egg pancake
debt a
Hume debt his head injured—
she sees I'm staring
at her boyfriend's arms

_____

we partner with a pig farm

———

think of pressing the faun
darkly from behind,
Marlo or Marlon we are
beholden to backward pressing

———

he chooses to wear
a T-shirt in 28-degree weather
to show off muscular arms
not just to his girlfriend
but to us, pestilences

———

 tonight I
will be the vulgate rememberer—
encouraging bubble mentality

———

using "mutter" wrongly in
a throttled story
and showing the story to
someone whose own
relation to power was throttled

———

bragging about *Beowulf*
in 1980—bragging about
Plutarch in 2016

———

never wanting to sit
near me because I'll be
gay flag unwriting his authority

———

    start reciting
the *Iliad* at the top of my lungs

———

they walk around
apartment wearing
kimonos and cock rings
and nothing else—
bear culture

———

Glenn Gould said
Streisand italicized

———————

your Baltimore
beard in diner
contrite booth

———————

again my mother's red
Parker ballpoint pen
by the downstairs wallphone

———————

son is a goldfish
with a veiltail boyfriend—
tetrachromatic suckers

———————

white address book featuring
Aunt Pearlie, not
partial to my mother

———————

not the redemptive fairy
I'd anticipated

———————

       in public library
I asked where are books
about doctors?
embarrassed to say
I sought *Doctor*
Zhivago—librarian
exiled me from
adult card catalogue
and deported me to kid
books about doctors

—————

       in my drawer
Elmer's glue, index cards,
hole puncher, rubber cement,
coin collection in a blue
cardboard folder—squeeze
pennies into blue holes

—————

he chose the object
because it was nearby—
I chose the object because
its carapace and numen

reminded me of an earlier
possession I was attached to

_____

        if the gown
drags, how can it
be absent? if it is
absent, how can it
be shining? and does
its dragging diminish
or exacerbate
the heart's irresoluteness?
(gloss on a stanza by
Benjamin Fondane)

_____

my body courted a siege
of Debbie Reynolds dolls
after her death by
stroke or broken heart
one day after her
daughter Carrie Fisher died

_____

my body locked
its emergency exits—
my body is a multi-volumed
Maigret escapade by
Edith Wharton or
a wedding
cookie sick of being
a wedding cookie

_____

a bathhouse
lice-carrier, photographed

_____

my body is a schwa
trying to achieve simultaneity
with Eddie Fisher through
whatever surgery is available

_____

may ink's
secret source
escape blame

_____

   listened to
last movement of Liszt
Faust Symphony—1960,
Leonard Bernstein,
tenor soloist Charles Bressler—
liner notes translate
chutzpadik Goethe's
Ewigweibliche
as "Woman in all of us"

————————.

contrite about the
thousand thresholds
each day I traipse
over without acknowledging
their momentousness

————————.

Walter Benjamin
refers to colporteurs
in his 1930
radio broadcast, aimed
at Berlin children—
I like Benjamin best

when he is speaking
to children about colporteurs
and puppet shows

————————

he mentions *Unter den Linden*—
to that "spot of time"
I may return, seeking
vainly to translate
the linden's askew
testimony, but don't
scorn me if sloth, fear,
or faithlessness
prevent my return

#33

[the cadavers resented us]

solitude, capers, Samantha
in *Bewitched,* Tarzan
remakes, constellations,
puce, ramekins—

—————————

who negates the lavender
flood?

—————————

butterfly expert
born in Moscow to parents
who spat on Lenin's
sister's grave

—————————

accused of lechery I
stand immune in a hatchet-
dominated corner of Fabian
Expressway, which runs

between Mars Canal and
Herbert von Karajan

———————

each phrase ignores its
neighbor in a *Divorce American
Style* scene I downloaded
in a funk

———————

    the nude
Honey I loved
then snubbed, refusing
to pay for his services

———————

    pilgrim
morsels climbed toward
Saturn in search of a hut

———————

dreamt I needed to pack
my luggage but had
too many toiletries and

no passport and no jurisdiction
over the hotel room

———————

after Debbie Reynolds died,
it was too late for her
to give thought to a world
without Debbie Reynolds

———————

       they were prime
cadavers, and "prime"
was a Warsaw
ghetto distinction bestowed
by church elders,
police, rabbis, my
father, your father,
every part of me
lined up at Marienbad's
airport

———————

       hungry,
we waited in line
to glimpse the cadavers

————————

the cadavers resented us

————————

any spell I fall under
I soon resent—I begrudge
hypnosis its hold

————————

blessed by a command from
an unseen source who long
ago told her not to care
that she would approach death
without redeeming her early
spectacular promises

————————

　　a few hours alone
with my gods so I can
destroy them, reinvent
them as goddesses

————————

you berate the measurer—

―――――

into decimals you break
the measurer, a puny
fossil you betrayed—you fold
your act of betrayal in half

―――――

in the old days, you
had wishes—you failed
to make good on them—
you, too, folded in half

―――――

      the wounds
deposited in your sons
take form in the scar
on your nose—a mark
of disfavor you've curried
with the measurer

―――――

mimic measurement
and measure mimicry

―――――

finger my nasturtium

_____

learn to isolate myself as
a nocturnal species

_____

imagine being a body
that gave birth 14 times

_____

because the last word
in the book was "green"
like Lorca

_____

Chabrol doesn't
conceal that Fabio
is much taller than
his male co-stars

_____

imagine Liz Taylor
killing a spider in her
bathroom

————

     begin to
hear implicit crevices
in the sounds of paper
folding and crinkling, chairs
groaning and squeaking

————

     like the teacher
who wrote for *National Geographic*
I drowned
my inattention
in cookies

————

     Walter Benjamin's
lost radio broadcasts,
no remaining script or score—
subjects included Robert Walser,
a visit to the copper works,
hashish, "the local
bar, an unexplored milieu"

————

fear of time moving and I
am not part of its movement

_____

I tried to decipher sky
messages above the deserted city

_____

Callas, pronounced
like college, collards,
colossal

_____

dreamt pale white deviant
family circus troupe
peered in my window—
one member, the most nude,
the most deviant, did suicidal
flips, handstands, somersaults—
a flesh-colored
leotard at the groin,
no indication
of gender—like an advertising
mannequin

————————

      backflips of the pale
nude deviant crossed the threshold
of safety and plausibility—
the observing parent figure
countenanced the ungainly
yet virtuoso backflips of
the son/daughter who found happiness
in this gymnastic-circus bubble
of bodily contortions

————————

worried about the back-
flipper's genital area—
its illegibility,
inscrutability, blankness—
diaper? poultice?

————————

      the backflipper
family's skin tone
bandage-white—
in bed I repeated
to myself "bandage-white"

314

#34

[the last guest]

      a makeshift
chauffeur took
us to a hill town

———————

we almost ran over a little
boy—our scooter
skirted him

———————

reading-orgy as
concentration exercise

———————

Dustin Hoffman a place
for Sam or sound
to visit all waffles—

———————

I did business
on top of waffles
I don't mind twisting

———————

color photo of Polish
girl killed at 14
in Auschwitz—before
the picture was taken
she dried her tears
and wiped her bloody lip

———————

    two hefty
condoms on sidewalk
outside parked truck

———————

    sourdough
rye *lieder*—
a beam, *abyme* it

———————

protesting tyrannic
exclusion of refugees—
Muslim ban

———————

letting
oneself be cruised, not assuming
we are considered ineligible

———————

the last guest missing—
how do you find
the statistically negligible last
guest? how do you determine
your own eligibility?

———————

Harry Mathews,
originator, died—

———————

Tiny Soap Operas

———————

fix a bloody spot
on the harlequin-boy's chin

———————

saw Sergei Eisenstein porno
drawings—bisexual

———————

the phrase "in spoons
I deposited my hopes"
arose—or "in a spoon I forfeit
my hopes"—but what
do spoons, hopes, and
forfeiture have in common?

———————

     toward Robert
Rauschenberg I rambled
but didn't reach him

———————

     pressing groins
in dream with Todd—
was I being reconsidered
for the *Vogue* stable?

————

I entered a beauty
salon that doubled
as a boutique's
changing room—
I asked "what genre
is this sweater?"

————

my pants had pleats
and flares—phares
penetrating my miasma

————

my *vogliatemi bene*
reply to his *Butterfly*
pocket proscenium shot

————

baby in pink T-shirt survived
vomiting spree

————

nun with casino sweatshirt
returns from the loo

       Fredric March
a quickie, Franchot Tone
a quickie, but I am
toneless and so don't qualify
for a quickie with Franchot

---

across the moat of his vanity
he says "you're looking good"

---

clustered gibbets—summit
giblets, knee gristle, octaves

---

       husband sealed
shut with duct tape

---

kid watching a snake video
animated on his father's iPhone

---

see a face in the filmed
wardrobe, garderobe,
Robespierre—sexual envy
of Robespierre with gap teeth
and a body he knows is ideal—
his smile confirms
the self-assessment

———————

spectralist chitchat—
Janis Joplin's posthumous messages

———————

my face begins to harden
and fall—an Eastern
European look-to-go—
order your Eastern
European look from the take-
out menu

———————

Martha Washington
and Dinah Washington
uncoupled though coincident

————————

a son, touching mother's unclad leg,
might be a neutered Manila
folder giving paper cuts
like Froot Loops to passersby

————————

wanting a different father
every night—not spin-the-bottle
but spin-the-philosopher

#35

[unseen ultramarine]

Siggy Freud urinating
on the fire to create civilization—
urine and the primal horde of guys,
low POV shot of incest campfire
with urinating Ur-fathers—
I'm three years old
looking up at civilization's
hoary, full-bladdered originators

—————

Freud almost ran
me over with his station wagon
outside the sunny café
where the man who can't walk
eats his breakfast every day
and at lunch holds court
over the lascivious typesetters

—————

be more open-minded, egalitarian,
generous toward the non-hot—

don't hubristically
strive for hotties

————

would rather get a Pulitzer
than be a dom—but I'll never
get a Pulitzer so
might as well be a dom—
an easy way to be victor
in my triumphal carriage,
faux-Napoleon of the moated grange

————

fathers retaining their fatherly
voices when they speak
to their young sons

————

what are the creeds
of the babysitters' cult?
where do they worship?
what sacred provisions
do they stockpile?

————

apology for demanding
a peanut butter and jelly sandwich
and then spitting it out

———————

Julie Andrews in *The Boy Friend,*
1954, eating a matzoh
piled with cheese

———————

     Gidget
makes water a tournament
of Gidget-refinement, becoming more
pop, more watery, more Gidget-
like—she isn't really Gidget
and she wants to become
Gidget, so she has to pretend
to be Gidget trying to become
more Gidget, when in fact
she is an imposter with
no relation to Gidget

———————

is she his mother or is she just
ogling him while she waits
to pee? I ate the Brie

———————

we discussed Adriana
Caselotti, Snow White's
voice in 1937

———————

　　　　shrimpy guy in North
House bed sophomore year,
my foot on his crotch
or his foot on mine
led to nothing more

———————

kid singing about marigolds
in tenth grade when marigolds
were a fad—everyone
was singing about marigolds

———————

his arm hair had grown back,
obscenely demonstrative rivulets

proving their unparaphrasable point—
I didn't finish my pierogis

—————

YouTube is the torn
place—a movie theater can
be the torn place—how to
tear is the question—rip,
shred, diversify, make
a single object *two* objects
by tearing it—don't tear it
completely, make
the tear superficial

—————

kid's orange plastic button
lying orphaned on the floor—
kid doesn't even notice
the orange plastic button—again
I become through repetition
the only one
alive to love the orange
plastic button abandoned
publicly on the agora

floor—worthless
place to roost

————————

      piercing we
are the impossible
fog—are we impossible
or is the fog
the culprit, if impossibility
is a crime?

————————

"I want Mommy now"
the little kid says
and the father says "you could die"

————————

appalling force the jet's air
maintains—how
is smoke torn?

————————

      difficult buttocks
in a balmy spring

———————

differentiate
celestial
protuberances

———————

the promiscuous unseen—
cuit means cooked—
is promiscuity the
uncooked promise
or the cooked promise
or the raw Prometheus
or the umami Prometheus?

———————

"gloaming," writes Didion—
brown weed-plain, desolation,
as if my grandfather had given
me this river-book

———————

tittering
falls or *Titicut Follies*

———————

dreamt of nude
bath with father—
skinny waist, butt pre-
dominating, strangely
S-shaped body, green sludge

———————

hillside house I rhapsodized
when my ideals were high

———————

      tunnels
and cumquats, my reflection
in ashtray's closed lid—
smoke cloud and then jumpcut
to suit, tie, rope,
zebra, the stripe foregone
and babysat for—

———————

to babysit a stripe with no
intention of aiding the stripe,
to lie bleeding on the pavement
because your stripe is amiss

————————

      columbarium
grotto divests cloud

————————

surge of desire for arm
video the drowsing
neighbor watches

————————

      the school
bus's attitude toward
destruction it causes

————————

      river hut,
ignored by wild rose—
hut, eager for flower's mute
accolades, rose's identity
stronger than mine

————————

the unseen afterlife
is promiscuous, or the fringes
of consciousness are promiscuous—

tomorrow, say more about why
the unseen is promiscuous

————————

          some mystic
in a New Haven
backyard spotted
the God personage suddenly
materialized—a ficus
beneath a sky too late
to qualify as ultramarine

————————

why characterize sight
as aggressive and curious?
why not imagine
sight as passive, expectant,
accepting whatever
bounty is thrown
to its cur-soul?

————————

notice now I'm calling
our plight a cur's

————————

cur incurious
because to seem
too curious would
offend the sky
we hope will return
to the ultramarine
that precedes absolute
night

————

      a thousand
stars puncture
your misgivings,
pierce your distrustful
sight-sickness,
and provide pinched
apertures for wording
everything differently
the next time we
make this voyage

#36

[the faux-ailing abacus] ·

sissy aqueducts
amoral aqueducts
introspective aqueducts

———————

      get accustomed
to the appearance of my
posthumous dwelling-place

———————

Celan's incommunicable
experience communicated

———————

frottage investigates
restful mind playing
Marsden Hartley's
"almost / loquacious skies"

———————

O to be
almost loquacious
rather than fatally
over loquacity's edge!

———————

June 27th
Anna Moffo's birthday
caro nome
three Blue Point oysters
eaten with precise poet

———————

     succulent's
shadow on white table,
Icelandic rocks on
pink cookie-plate

———————

defrocked minister
flirtatious

———————

white hydrangeas
are a crowd—under

their populous face
I shine, overdosing

————————

whipped cream
had a hard time
surrendering to the whip

————————

     age and
hydrangeas cast laden
shadow on blue
pen-box, orange
striated cup

————————

erect white-green
hydrangeas, green
informs and infuses
your white, complicates
and undoes it—
teal reflected
light cast
upward from jar
an undecidable

place between blue
and green

————————

       because
your dress was teal
I didn't see you,
you blended into the room—
after you said "hello"
you diverged
from sofa and columns—
a moment earlier
your teal dress
had undermined
your claim to
a separate existence

————————

Toscanini didn't approve
of Callas's diction

————————

       skinny sauna-
haunter, basso,
never says hello

_____

ass in Ithaca
mirror looked
unattractively speed-bumpy

_____

granaried in a hornbook

_____

I decided to end
the essay with three
Portuguese words

_____

her words themselves
aren't the source
of pain—it's what
happens to my body
when I hear her voice

_____

the clock's face
communicates
uncommunicativeness—
one word fills

the bucket, and
I'm the bucket

———————

I said "sixteen"
when I woke up—
what did sixteen mean?

———————

what herbs in the tea
coarsened consciousness?

———————

apotropaic, the power
to ward off—Atropos
is deviant

———————

gnarled gnosis
garlanded gargoyle

———————

desiring spacious
liberties tampered with

by stone statue
sinned upon by Mars
and Venus collaborating
on moonlight's
shivering projects

————————

is Chaplin's terra firma
the same as Buster Keaton's?

————————

is Shakespeare reclaiming
his sod from the same
manufacturer I'm reclaiming
my sod from?

————————

I groped language
because I had nothing
else to grope

————————

        and if language
disappears forever

on what ground
will I stand?

_____

ungoverned aspects
of Peter Quint?
you could be forced
to dwell inside the
name Quint,
and Quint would
begin to define you—
an almost-affair with
Peter Quint dressed up
as Serendipity
the *bâtarde cantatrice*
of Offenbach will-o'-
the-wisp fame

_____

Mathieu
Lindon, who fell
in love with Hervé
Guibert and lived
or crashed in

Foucault's apartment,
fancies Offenbach

———————

dramatic soprano
at 90 can sing
Lorenzo Da Ponte's
diaphanous aria

———————

Ashbery turns 90
this month—topless
photo of young J.A.

———————

        spotted
kind—to spot
(freckle) kindness,
to turn kindness, a formerly
solid property,
into speckles

———————

a perplexed,
cotton-fed abacus—

imagine the abacus
has a mouth and
a nurse is stuffing
the abacus-mouth
with cotton—
the abacus wants calf's
liver or goose liver
but the nurse insists
that the ailing abacus
eat cotton

———————

I am the faux-ailing
abacus, and the melodrama
starring the abacus
is bereft of orchestra—
who in the pit
will accompany
cotton-fed *sanglots*?

———————

      Saturday
morning trumpet-
vines an orange
approaching fire-engine red

————

owl slept in porch
nook—shy, nearly
dead? difficult
to verify it was an owl—
ailing owls curl
into themselves, become
orbicular

————

purple astilbe
in shade—clematis
huge against shadowed
pine, bereft
of bunny—ornamental
cherry tree 17
years bigger
than when I first
met it—did I
ever meet the pear tree?

————

Éditions
de Minuit I now
understand—midnight's

minotaur—no sun
suddenly—a "v"
inside the angular
knife-chirp of a local
bird—behind
the individual chirp
is a looser orchestra
of various tumbled-
together bird songs and
cars on Route 9G

—————

      canna,
orange tall flower,
three cups pinned
to the same faucet—
a tree of bone
china demitasses
tinted orange for
punishment's sake

—————

dream of old man tumbling,
uncontrollable somersaults
down E train

53rd Street stairs—
then tumbling
onto the subway's
third rail, then
tumbling beyond
visibility—the tumbling
disease—he's OK
until the urge hits,
but once he begins
to tumble he can't stop—
death-wish tumbling
tropism

_____

tumbling's violence
overtook him and placed
him outside the circle
of my empathy

_____

ceasing to empathize
with the tumbling man
was a sin I dress
up as an inevitability

_____

origins of totalitarianism
are scattered in my book—
read it to divine
World War Three

———————

if I interpret the wooden
nipple to death, I can
marry the rabbi—
we can interpret
the nipple together—
the rabbi and I
can foment an orgy
of interpretation

———————

German Romanticism
killed its pets

———————

we interpret
the things we love
to death, and thereby
we amass knowledge—
Wissenschaft

————————

      turquoise
contains more green
than I remember

————————

      your chin
is regally square
I told the harpsichordist

————————

ultramarine blue
Flashe vinyl paint
underlies the layers
of figuration that
come next—
you can't see
the ultramarine underlayer,
but it makes possible
the lines that seem
to be the bottom
layer but are
secretly the top

#37

[grunt bouillon, cupcake mannerisms]

      lavender
vestibule, below stairs,
where the Frank O'Hara
purple Pierrot used to hang

_____

      regret stone wall
by Narcissus pool

_____

failing the Pilates instructor by
not consummating the marriage

_____

      Soupy Sales
and Don Rickles are
my peer group—sludge
of Don Rickles identification

_____

buy a slinky shirt—
demand that it be louche

———————

infinitesimal green bug
jumped—limited
love I could drum up
for the green bug

———————

neutralize a painful tendency,
give exact names to dismal
phenomena—P.E. shame,
trying to throw a ball

———————

    fodder for
incestuously investigative
fashion show qua thought
camp

———————

    under supervision
I sit in sunny seminary

coign as a single
isolated specimen, never
lumped into quorum
or majority

———————

summer consciousness
sparkler-stillborn,
juvenile fireworks

———————

    white hydrangea
acquired nervy
stem's sapphire tint

———————

hair like a confirmation
hat—confirming what?
this jetty onto the body
of my mother's op-art friend

———————

third-grade girl's
flat resistant face
knowing I rejected her—

shakes her head, the curls
bounce, but her expression
doesn't change

_____

sang about Wolf Man
a tergo penises on tree

_____

                    pangolin
in danger of extinction
is Marianne Moore's possession

_____

leaving flowers on Ridiculous
Theater doorstep the day
after Charles Ludlam died

_____

        stationary rock
frozen in its failure
to be a flowing waterfall—
green spears, white
phlox, orange canna

_____

grunt bouillon

————————

hummingbird flirting
with trumpet vines—white
butterfly making
the acquaintance of nascent
clematis—now butterfly
befriends rudbeckia

————————

          "cheet"
says sparrow or lark,
a long "cheet"
like "chie-iet," the second
syllable higher in pitch,
and then a general
background chorus of "hallelujah!"—
now the white butterfly,
companionable as a silent dog,
courts lavender and hyssop

————————

plumbago
striving to exceed its pot

———————

*Night of the Living
Dead* George
Romero died

———————

my nipples point downward
not outward

———————

succulent undulates
on small canary plate—
sunflowers in cobalt pitcher—
shells (gleaned near Búðir's lava rocks)
on flamingo dish—succulent's
member rises—no, its ascending
branch nearly
touches the sunflower's pendant
green leaf but doesn't arrive—
Yahweh's flirtatious
distance from Adam

————

      "castrated,"
a woman at the diner said
three times, firmly—
adamantine or diamantine
writing continuing to pursue
its even edge—sedge
selvage salvages savage
sausage *sauvage savoir*
saveur savior signor
signals significance

————

dreamt two tiny spiders
in rhubarb clafoutis

————

disappear from the sexual
agora into a matrimonial cloud

————

"Susan Lecturing
on Neitzsche" [sic]
—painting by Paul Thek, 1987

———————

           free croissant
I refused while listening
to Etta James

———————

Etta Cone, conehead, head
me toward Coney Island
where I can research
freaks of Madison
High where my
mother wanted to go—
she went to Abraham
Lincoln instead

———————

three days ago was Walter
Benjamin's 125th birthday

———————

again recalling
safety-seeking
father's toothbrush
and pens in his
shirt's front pocket

————

straight couple
making out on subway
platform—she wearing
a white/black horizontally
striped dress—he
wearing a brown hat
like mine, but mine
is blue—his hat's rim
shallower

————

ORLAN,
artist specializing
in facial alteration

————

swam
in lane next to extremely
skinny father (a medical
case?) and his skinny son—
the son's skinniness doesn't
look pathological

————

dreamt that Steve brought
a friend home from the gym—
his name was Spinoza—
he lay, clothed, on our bed

—————

Jeanne Moreau died—
downturned lip,
shadow-ringed gaze

—————

      tattoo on bicep
says stark, stack,
track, or back—
back from hell?

—————

      Charlotte Brontë,
a book about birds,
her father's cataracts—
opportune moment to start
writing a novel is when your
father submits to surgery

—————

Sartre's
cupcake mannerisms

————

Penelope Fitzgerald's
The Blue Flower and
although I am the star
of *Boom!* I have never
properly read Novalis

————

pocket park's
rudbeckia observed
by father whose extreme
skinniness catalyzes
medical curiosity

————

despite
peril, gum
chewer urges me to jump
into his vermilion void

#38

[consecrate my life to cucumber]

flesh swirl removed
from large grapefruit

———————

kissing couples,
stare of a curator
who is not Thoreau
in Tuscany

———————

pay a house call
to Ogden Nash with
radium poisoning—
practice *messa di voce*

———————

I'm not incest-hungry
Elisabetta but whipper-
snapper gay
Adriana Lecouvreur out on boy's

night, Sacramento
meat-eater at heart

———————

sitting listless with
mother while she advances
through her chocolate pudding

———————

      tree creates
drawable outline against
bracketed window—
"to bracket" is a phrase
not widely understood

———————

terrified about nuclear
showdown with North Korea

———————

Pink Sands air
freshener in car
to Truly Mediterranean

———————

Marcel Pagnol is now
my best friend—we
had rum and cokes together
the last night of
the Bakelite crossword
Charlotte Salomon festival—
I won the César
for Best Charlotte
Salomon crossword
puzzle solver—
I used a hopefulness
laxative in my studio
above the liquor store

_____

car salesman golfer
geezer in *South
Pacific* founds
Pauline Kael
Pauline Oliveros fan club

_____

sunburned
with a beige purse,

Ellen Terry please
come home

————————

at Niagara Falls
we discussed colonizing
bacteria, under-
rated complexity of a sad
potato connected to
Elaine Stritch's
"everybody rise"

————————

sinking into errata
snippets in a high-
ceilinged Degas—
footprint of dad's
crush on fireside
"Desiderata"

————————

    my mother
got an A+ from
I.A. Richards because

she contradicted him
in the final exam—
immortal and controversial
blue book like a blue-
bottle fly caught
in Dickinson's retina

———————

a chaser father
to bring you closer
to the *poire belle Hélène*
dessert father

———————

Pembroke Pines,
where my grandparents met
appetizing deli death

———————

she harmonized The Who
with *Games People Play*—
child welfare laws
people play, spoiled
fruit people play

364

————

a long neck like the
precocious cocksure
masturbator lost
in translation—
gâteau errors,
slots of grammar's
interchangeability thrill
me on a side street

————

books are
buckets—a snort
of Jimmy Cagney

————

goodbye,
world, perishable
envelope of DNA,
oxygen, salubrious
pollen

————

poveri fiori Renata
Tebaldi fears vulgarity—
desolate roadhouse
rocks with pucker-holes

———————

once I could seduce
by wearing white
bucks, khakis,
pink shirt—Liz kiss
associated forever
with donut shop

———————

Advent calendar version
of pleasure's pop-up
infrequency
and my relation (un-
consummated Jocasta)
to veronica as
salve or abortifacient

———————

two pickles,
Bobby Darin and Sandra Dee,
anorexia and depression

———————

consecrate my
life to cucumber

———————

the perfect lipstick
is pragmatism

———————

morsels from
The Doctor's Wife—
cellarage
specky potatoes
greengage tart
pleasaunce
coke-ashes
bar-parlour
wood-anemones
vampire-trap

———————

a moron rules the world—
nothing we can
do about it?

———————

my renascent freakishness
matches the TV star's

———————

       I sauerkraut
thee twice

———————

confessed to bedwetting
while we chewed hamburger
flamboyantly without bun—
and thus a hamburger
grows illegible to itself

———————

dreamt that dignified
women urinated on a gym
bathroom's floor

———————

I side with plagiarists
who pretend to treat
their narcissism ironically

_____

      my turned-out
right foot, father watching
me walk—was he
dissatisfied with my height?

_____

please resuscitate
lemon-spice visiting cake
as category of pleasure

_____

circle of hostile light
ellipses on disposable
palette I should photo-
graph before I destroy

#39

[lax hug]

slow bumpy inscription
on moonlit paper bag,
umber ink almost invisible—
no crime to enjoy
impediment

_____

conch shell's masochism

_____

flyaway Tammy Grimes
hair I'm not allowed
to mention

_____

how did she burn
her hand on crumpets?
and do the gristle bits
in crumpet dough
foil her designs?

————

I wanted
to waylay the drudge
in his cubicle
to receive a lax hug—
what makes a hug lax?

————

noticed an orange
door—burnt
orange? also a
strange calligraphic
insignia on a building's
distressed surface—
a chicken joint

————

long ago I asked
"is Lana Turner a monad?"

————

monad, meme, martyr

————

loneliness of long-distance
non-*frum frum*-chaser

_____

able to survive
at 110 years old

_____

those lakes I thought
were women's bodies
are actually clouds—
those clouds I thought
were women's bodies
are actually lakes

_____

we hover in cloud
cover—cloud covers what
with its opacity? cloud
covers loquacious
questioning

_____

      wrongly rumored
glass eye of Sandy Duncan

_____

finding white dry
crumbs in ear-fold
treasure-repositories

_____

Sontag's *Death Kit*
discarded from Macalester
College library—not
checked out in five years

_____

aggressively correct pronunciation
of *Trastevere*

_____

he didn't seem sufficiently
excited that I was also a Virgo

_____

cloud wisps like *National
Velvet* over North Carolina hill
winding lake-roads
resembling vase-rims

—————

Tante Alice suitcases still
in closet, or discarded?

—————

throw out dead neighbor's
manual Smith-Corona
or save it? write poems
on dead neighbor's typewriter?
she who muttered
"keep going" in gym
while lifting and lunging

—————

we spoke excited French
on Martin Luther King Jr.
Boulevard on way to crêpe shop

—————

Kirk's Steakburgers, mother
sitting aloof at her own
table—did she often eat
separately from us?

—————

plot empowers denizens
gathered ungregarious
on violent lawn where no
banshee in furniture
finds repetition hollow

———————

Christmas music sacralizes
sauna timbrels ungauzing
Cassandra's wet suit
misapplied toward beatitude

———————

history dismembers rabbis
postulating febrile-minded
Crete-derived fondue
forks skewered into waves

———————

skirmish until snouts grown
Romanesque stampede

———————

Capulet her
or rotunda him

———————

rotunda hymn,
robotic tampering

———————

repose soap pony

———————

after kissing guys
two times, he realized
he wasn't attracted to stubble

———————

lip balm stick peeping
out my left pocket

———————

seduction, education, ducats—
to deduce a Ducati

———————

Shahryar sometimes saw
Sophia Loren wandering
around Geneva lake

————

have I stamina
for syntax-cradle?

#40

[her favorite antidepressant is tofu]

Bette Davis on Dick Cavett
regrets the self-
destructiveness of "Miss Garland"

———————

intestinal growl—
white tulips more
intact than their red brethren

———————

reading Cortázar too quickly
without looking at Spanish original

———————

my gut's loud violence—
the same leonine guys
lined up, none available

———————

not gessoing the board—
enjoying Masonite's hardness

————————

and my stone-inhibited mouth
in avuncular circumference

————————

      my belly
biting itself—
drainage towelette

————————

this seismic
sectioning's
a love-act

————————

vampire-trap provoked commentary
but greengage tart did not—
of sumps I am a devotee

————————

outline on white table
is a ball finding a path
apart from its gewgaw sister

———————

cock has become pencil taped to spindle
showing off independence
and playpen with brother
learning to walk, a happening
already seized and pilloried

———————

Kandinsky moment in silver-bordered
window, the Calder ellipse
a drama I depict but fail to narrate

———————

blinded by sun reflected
off meringue building—
loving the unreciprocating entrepreneur's
phallic remorselessness

———————

touched by reverse tulips—
petal's capacity to tuck me *up,*
a darker swoon inside pistil

———————

Rose Kennedy in my dream
discussing cleaning supplies—
she praises *unheimlich* detergents

—————

she thinks Kurt Weill
is the origin of unhousing
or the unhouseful

—————

penis is a blank spot—
I get more traction with testicles

—————

heart is also blank—
it either grows invisible
or clamors for attention

—————

tongue, lips, mucous membranes
unhappily segmented

—————

I tried
to describe Hedy Lamarr's modernity—
her resemblance to Merle Oberon

_____

the explanation contained
too many instances of the words *have*
and *has*—she *has* thoughts,
we *have* been thinking

_____

bottom purple edge
contains a cup-shaped absence
revealing wood underneath

_____

put fingers deep into clay-potato
as she instructed—
I plunged my hand
into her orange pool

_____

white birch tree's
line between thin

window-blind slats not
coinciding with brown
building's grid

———————

withered outsider
petal's diffidence

———————

utter the cut stalely—
state the cut
slated for demolition

———————

her favorite antidepressant
is tofu

———————

white rooftop of Corfu
across the street is a new
repeated mood door

———————

                    repeat
the lava dance upon the stuck
scolded mirror

————————

nosebleed in restaurant—
shivering ungainly petal,
outward horizon of intact
housebroken tulip

————————

she too with her hobo
nervousness—beef stew
repeating the failure to agree

————————

say yes, say no,
and you cum on the no's
downbeat

————————

she and the thousand others died—
"piling up the instances"—

———

but where is the pile
and what are the instances?

#41

[tumbling cheese, the umpteenth scissoring]

mother's dresses
sister's dresses
touch his curls

————————

bluefish making noises

————————

dreamt crazy man
threw an indigent
mocked man
in a wheelchair over
an atrium railing

————————

I observed the transition
from *jeu d'esprit*
to catastrophe

————————

I misheard "She's
A Burglar" (song)
as "she's a pergola"

——————

dreamt I wrote with
orange lipstick
two words from Beckett's
The Unnamable—
cang, cenotaph

——————

cang = wooden yoke
worn for punishment

——————

cenotaph = monument marking
a grave, though the remains
are buried elsewhere

——————

write a poem
describing the intersection
of cang and cenotaph

————————

last night the coldest
in 100 years

————————

mother says
her usual time for
labor was 1 a.m.—
a spinal for pain—
I arrived at 6 a.m.—
birth she says
was easy

————————

proving "the fallibility
of my face"

————————

  identifying
with upright purple vase
and yellow flowers outlined
punctiliously in blue

————————

violent and non-
empathic act of saber-
judgment—not saber
as in taste or knowledge
(*savoir, saber*) but
saber as in curved
thought-blade
reason-knife

————————

grandfather's unpublished
unread manuscript on
Jews in American literature,
handed me by grandmother
with no instructions—
dilemma of a bequest
unexplained

————————

affixing scraps
haphazardly to a found
wood slab
without choreographing
his pleasures

I misread
"the power of
design" as "the poetry
of despair"

----

dreamt disabled
woman became nude
as she tumbled
down an escalator—
at first she tried to walk
with a cane but then
realized it was impossible
to manage individual steps—
easier to roll, to tumble—
echoing my earliest-read
fairy tale's tumbling cheese
wheel that rolled from town
to town—Bremen? Munich?

----

the woman lost
her clothes as she tumbled
down the escalator

————

after playing
the *Pathétique* Sonata
I ate all the lentil
soup's pancetta,
insufficiently rendered

————

futile chat
with masochist,
his dick in a chastity cage

————

Hostess apple
turnover, large and not good
but I keep eating it

————

dreamt mother returned
to her sold house for a few
last days of life

————

half a dead dry
pretzel lying on Eighth
Avenue pavement

———————

red fire hydrant
spoke annunciation to me—
a jetty, her Smith-Corona berth
upstairs, ecru accordion
door closing

———————

guard the umpteenth scissoring

———————

green pillars doubling
as neap tide's fluorescent orange
"hep" horseshoe-
stache clone

———————

    snack
your way to Dover

———————

    lactating
uncle in dream had
gay inklings, opera adulation,
Philomela or Ptolemy

————

cruelty to Bible instructor—
as if our mirthful sadism
mattered more than
the Pentateuch

————

no reciprocation
from college 69 mate—
his low voice in common
room entered my heart along
a path that didn't exist
until his timbre forged it

————

another village higher
than I can reach, though
15 years ago I
could have attained it—
vertical striations
in ice edifice

————

their feeble coupled entrance
into corner restaurant

————————

two geese and lone flag
near academy
inculcating nothingness

————————

surfer's
prerogative to consider
ocean wave an arctic
mountain wearing a baseball
cap of foam

————————

download an Iceland
photo to send the masochist

————————

glean
acclaim from river-dwellers?
soft wheat-pillows for
gleaner-heads in five
pleated inconsequential rows

————————

when you never make a pass,
that lacuna is a never-pass

———————

he said she said I didn't
know how to kiss, and we agreed—
but who is we?
a mountain has the smiling
capacity to transform
my ice into her "I"

———————

Isolde's prelapsarian chill—
kayak with Isolde on
YouTube down a thin
estuary, pop-
ulated by bamboo prostheses—
Macbeth's fear of estuaries

———————

pie-wedge
ruby lines intact—emerald
enviable *Schloss*

———————

lime and coal, what
is their relationship?
am I the lime in the family?

———————

glean
Hayley Mills on Broadway—
glean man-head framed by
rectangular window reflection

———————

to remain
a theoretical gleaner
abstaining from the actual

#42

[puberty interruptus, a fairy burden]

masochism is decorative,
not a load-bearing element

————

into the graveyard
I dipped my demand

————

pile of slattern wooden
platforms painted blue—
rusty trestles, unloved

————

ambiguous dead leaves or
chrysanthemums not decorative,
addressing with their profusion
the plight of the dead branch

————

shale, no friend
of mine goes near you

————

if dandelions could sing
instead of disperse

————

   I forego
my crabbiness and the stones
shoulder the blame,
enriched thereby

————

why characterize myself as
the most monstrous defector?

————

the open poem
of winter

————

   being rejected
is a brine—
brined, I become
modern, like Modigliani

————

two strangers told
me I looked like Woody
Allen—another asked
"are you Jewish?"

———————

the assoanus, Vita
Sackville-West tells me,
is a miniature narcissus

———————

sun on piled-up
scrap metal

———————

       fox didn't
want to say yellow though I
aimed every morsel at him—
soft wet lip and a body
willing to be held

———————

brine sex grotesquerie
of the always depicted—
develop glossary of shapes

————————

    she oft
brought up duxelles—
a 1981 fixation

————————

a French man whose
steady application of hand
to page surpasses mine

————————

met a young bisexual writer
today for tea—we discussed
fraternity hazing
and fingernail polish

————————

goodbye, U.S. exceptionalism,
a Baskin-Robbins ice cream flavor
it's time to take off the market

————————

dreamt I scratched
my neck and nose
to make them bleed

_____

a boy too small
to use a urinal
was nonetheless led
to this unreachable,
mature fixture

_____

expert said my house's
tap water had an undertaste
of swordfish—no time
to make a proper
inspection to verify her intuition

_____

dreamt I read aloud
to a toddler-boy
a story that included
the word *critic*—
I told the kid's mother
he didn't yet know the word—
we agreed to make
recitation a counting exercise
("how many people are in

this photograph?") to avoid
contaminating his young mind

————

in the front row
Anna Moffo and
a credulous chauffeur—
Eddie Fisher or Sal Mineo—
I tried to explain
my momentary blindness

————

power of unkemptness
to soul-murder the passerby

————

holding "writing" far away
from me because it is
a cone, a V, volume not line—
I fall asleep *into* the cone
and permit its V
to dominate me

————

holding the door shut
with his leg, and I criticize
him for blocking
the nugatory door—outdated
alchemies of syllable

————

lint-covered
woman at kiosk
shakes leg

————

knock on Oz
outhouse door,
her banana
a security breach—
find baked goods for sale
in a privy converted
to a home furnishings boutique

————

      slowly knitting
a yellow nothing

————

"clutch" she said as if
"clutch" were a revered life-surge—
I was disgusted by its sound
or by her reliance on its power—
horror of being placed
(Lucky Pierre) between
her regard for clutch
and its dominating nature

———————

no escape from clutch—
to be clutched by her familiarity
with clutch's new, raw
salience

———————

clutch circum-
scribed me within
a magic circle
of dubiousness—
I could sit within clutch's
bow-and-arrow viewfinder
and receive the sting
of clutch's cupid-dart—

———————

I overheard
clutch's relevance—
clutch, a cited fact, like
retching or revolution

———————

if clutch was unimpeachably
true, why was clutch
the center of my
dubiousness? the red-hot
poker that defined me
as a not-god?

———————

clutch was the helpmeet
of a more tempestuous origin—
I joined their suicidal seance

———————

I craved
thunder and mistook
the clutch-sovereign
for storm-symptom,
the partial town, not wooded

————————

       and the partial face,
hiding, renounced
or denounced for being a noun
in hiding, or for hiding
my loathed nouns

————————

cash in on Mr. Rochester's sexiness,
then shudder away the identification—
if I get called "it,"
shudder to extirpate
the cruel designation—
populace receiving
my porn-tutelage,
a born porn-Tudor

————————

       dreamt I sat
in the front row at the Met,
Gioconda—the soprano reached forward,
poked my eyes and gave
me an unwanted hand-job

————————

dreamt painter
heard through mistaken
scuttlebutt that in a lecture
about his art I'd said
"he owns the laundromat"

———————

painter resented that I brought
economy into the discussion—
in circles I tried to justify
a comment I couldn't
recall making

———————

remembering when
a poet, now dead,
called me an "easy lay"

———————

paralysand = paralyzed
analysand

———————

playing keno
with catheter-grandfather
strep throat team-tagged

————————

gummy
bear collaborations, tasting
the Internet-shaft's thickness,
Barbizon Hotel honey
in grippe of forensic
Firenze Fiorucci
Ferenczi frenzy

————————

lemon-singer
like *Meistersinger*
or BLT-singer

————————

Pandora's mountain-mind
would rather look away
from gastronomy and observe
random cluttered kink

————

like hats or has-beens,
ocular wizardry polishing
my Manhattan ginger
foursome—four otters
crashing into four
pastel ranch houses

————

    Mister Rogers
blames me for puberty
interruptus, a fairy burden—
a few squad cars
or a fey squire or fancy dress
ball for *Baumkuchen*
lovers, straight consumers
of spit cake

————

can't find a decent image
to send the masochist—
he wants a photo
that will decimate
his ego, already in tatters

#43

[know-it-alls in pilly cardigans]

trouble with loud
voice, trouble with
lost decades,
trouble with cast
of mind that consigns
a decade to the
category of "lost"

————————

type up a revenge
poem against guys
who've rejected
or ignored me—
call it "The Pathos
of Communication"

————————

is writing frenetically
by hand a form
of aerobic exercise?

————————

butter didn't walk
away after the
wedding, brick
by brick butter
didn't walk away

———————

     difficult
powerful pacifier
in player-baby
mouth—toddler
actress messing
up at Neiman Marcus

———————

emphatic operatic
speech of know-it-alls
in pilly cardigans

———————

autumn eyelashes is
certain he has decades
of seduction ahead of him,
while I have five acres

of absence under
my sweater

————————

how to work up
big loads to
impress the laity

————————

conversation is
often disgusting,
an excuse for one
self to smear
itself over other
selves, to congeal
unformed interiority
into premature
Jell-O-like faux-solidity—
stay liquid
and internal, don't
reify your thoughts
into aspic

————————

one by one
the cuties gather
outside the former
copy shop

———————

cockroach catcher
behind doctor's
examining table

———————

sinking into drawing
or drawing into
sinking—unlock
the contrition
underneath the praised
balustrade

———————

sound of a woman
walking versus
sound of a man

———————

holes within
tacit observation

————

take pink away
from its eagerness
to erase green

————

Santa-costumed
motorcyclist on
Van Ness, radio
blaring Sister Sledge's
"We Are Family"

————

watching *Marjorie Morningstar*
on the nursing-home TV
to savor Natalie Wood
acting Jewish

————

idea for essay—
"Orality in the

Pre-Socratics"—
no research,
no bibliography,
plenty of apocrypha
and innuendo

———————

sang "Avant de quitter"
from Gounod's *Faust* today,
replacing the libretto's words
with *knee*, *thee*,
V, *they*, and *nay*

———————

wiping
blurred prepositions

———————

"syncretic" she
says in New Orleans,
Catholicism and
mom mixed
in with heat and
Frenchness like

deviled eggs and
accidentally shaved
Brussels sprouts
orderly yet akimbo

———————

today William
Corbett died—
long ago he wrote me
a letter kindly
diagnosing my sonnet's
Lord Weary condensation

———————

    slamming
words together
until the words hurt
like damaged tin-
type, cakes
baked in tin

———————

fascinated by the
dead Kabbalah

on my delighted
arm I wrote
the concept of
festivity—how
societies fail

_____

dead person can
enter you on subway—
ghost settles
into its theory-
tune, an effigy
for excess, not a
play with trimmings

#44

[margarine a maritime latrine]

anonymous
not a Miss
not amiss
knot amiss

—————

above high C
Mr. Freud make me
your sex slave
on the couch

—————

Monica Vitti +
my Olivetti

—————

how to make
love to a monster
through any orifices you
can find on his
monster body

———————

I took a photograph
of art writer's
forearm because
I liked his tattoo

———————

a Citroën named desire

———————

on her lunch break
Liz brakes for men
and women on Planet 9

———————

how does Liz have
the fortitude to brake
for near-death
citizens of Planet 9?

———————

even if I gave
Paul Thek a blow
job, he wouldn't
attend this party

———————

snow is general across Ireland
means start thinking
universally
unless you're a monad
orgy oleander traitor

———————

      German music
in my father's head
as he got off the boat

———————

if Liz onstage
had a conniption fit

———————

if you want to
practice the arts
of the grave,
follow me

———————

      a kitsch-
monger on the sly

I blew a guy named
Nick Schnell
nicht schnell
not fast
my grade-school crush

————————

Brahms
hubbub in the hammam

————————

my puberty's
comestible Marie
Antoinette decapitation
return to 1969 when
Love, American Style
premiered

————————

Molotov cocktail
in the key of
Dorian Gray

————————

knock on the wooden
nipple's door—
annotate the nipple

———————

autophagia's
cadence of capitulation
isn't revolution

———————

maybe the rabbi himself
has a wooden nipple

———————

eructation of Zola
if Zola were Carmen

———————

a lark ascends
in marijuana's
eternal *aiuto*!

———————

Mitridate Mithridates
miter dented by *mater*

is tub margarine
a maritime latrine

—————

and how sensory is your urine
nadir-dwellers
I awed it
or it awed me
awed is a bed
a wedding is bleeding

—————

to be suddenly
Pessoa considered
small or Hart Crane
considered centrifugal

—————

write a faux-genealogy
of how it disappears

—————

hesitate before
criticizing the artist

who died at 36—
retract and revise
the too hasty dismissal

_____

a scholar says
"objects always withdraw"—
why do objects withdraw?
is withdrawal unique
to objects?

#45

[butter-colored slacks and rubber rum balls]

melancholy produces
doubling and linguistic
self-consciousness

————————

step by step toward
nonce proof—
never gliding

————————

as if Renata Tebaldi and David Cassidy
desired mayhem—
Blow Job and *Blow-Up*
fracturing the visible

————————

David Cassidy
with complications
and a wartime detail
about your identity

————————

five words
Alice James uses
not in your
customary vocabulary

————————

tactile reading
with eyes as haptic organ

————————

take a common object—
material or immaterial—
describe it—
describe it again

————————

no need to make it
literature—
just lay it out

————————

Poulenc's "halo of pedals,"
voice's clarity against

suddenly dissonant
temporary sweetness you're afraid
will engulf you

———————

Sophie Calle's
address and email
written down here

———————

tonality's
coronation

———————

don't tell of a world
out there—focus attention
on unspecific, unscrolling
consciousness right here

———————

a consciousness *of* and *about*
objects, but also consciousness
itself as pleasure and peril

———————

             overcoming
resistance to the process
as it unfolds, unaccustomed
language taking over

————————

America, an idea
hatched and held
in Europe

————————

Stein died in 1946—
think of people
you know or knew
who were alive in 1946

————————

butter-colored
slacks and rubber
training pencils

————————

serenely they chose
grave smell

mere grave
pansy hauntings

_____

vertigo of too many nuances—
don't drown in their rapidity—
choose the nuances you love
and settle down with them

_____

lovers know
the drawn figure gilded
a Berlin loaf of *Landbrot*

_____

consciousness
narrows, lubricates
unhappy amplitude

_____

book's bulk
killed the kid

_____

dog humping
shipwrecked object
or creature

_____

"she looked and looked"
and "thank you"
are lesbian signs

_____

Amb<u>ass</u>adors
am bad
doors *d'or*
bores into the lacunae
of the And

_____

hinged
intention's
not the same
as fixed purpose

_____

all is what was left over—
mind performing as record needle
resuscitating the all

———————

rum balls with powdered sugar
illustrating to the young
mouth the sometimes
unwelcome nature of a neighborliness
we now look back to
as sentimental apex
enclosed in rough paper lunch-bag

———————

door-to-door gift
of noisy maybe abusive
loving proximate seemingly
omniscient matriarch battling
her daughter

———————

       and we,
housed in language yet standing
outside words, watched

the husbanded fragment
of 1967 or 1972
gradually disappear

_____

we cling to the recollection
without valuing it

_____

nothing returns to us now
but the rumor of the fight
and the rum ball's hovering
on the precipice between
deliciousness and inedibility

_____

Mrs. S. gave us rum balls
among other treats
that weren't quite treats
is a more straightforward
way to frame the fable

#46

[chop up a sugary book]

penis-proportion of vitrine
space between logs

_____

write a novel about
relations between objects

_____

space between wall
text and object
is a psychotic fissure

_____

her side-of-toast sadism—
is she drinking chocolate
milk or prune juice at the bar?

_____

        chop up
a sugary book and find

compartmentalized pleasure-
zones inside it—in April
chop up the ginger book,
lemon-juice book also
cruelly segmented thus
becomes beef

———————

curled line
of beard-edge against baby-
fine skin and sleeve
arm tattoo an aqua-
marine toucan

———————

human autonomy killed
by piped-in music

———————

waking to Adam's mouth—
discovering the cultural
presuppositions of Adam's
mouth—write down
the lemon water's pour

but avoid *pour* because
it is minor and induces
"hit me" fear

_____

      human
variousness equals
a "hit me" syncopation—
to be swatted
by variousness

_____

the hyphenated noun-
phrase dialogic and gulping

_____

babies kill rumination
but aren't intentionally murderous—
superstitiousness
of unconsciously violent
guidance-counselor babies
making prophylactic
phone calls badly

_____

            "I want
to be a sex shaman"—
declared over shrimp
quesadillas

———————

I want to kick—
desire to kick not
pathological

———————

can a president explode
from excessive lying?

———————

        fuck-*Tod*—
to fuck death a radio
hunger aphorism

———————

Saul Bellow's finger
puppets

———————

π pi
runs away, I
bring back extinction—
light hits moored
fragment-boat and makes it
a lateral lisper, reprinted

———————

interested fists herding
my sculpted hills

———————

abrupt
leaf-stall—*Christstollen*
is eavesdropper cauldron

———————

an *After Dark*
dancer seeking slaw
in Warsaw

———————

St. Louis
dropping his soap-granola
in TV-shower

———————

I used to live 24
lines away from Rilke's bedsit

———————

shy cater-
wauling lox-caterer

———————

      home for debris-
groom accomplice

———————

expired pink shirt low
cut—a new
generation's tested
tuchus

———————

28 beards in school
pregnancy when you hit
lake water

———————

take a whisk
broom to lake water,
orchestrate it,
make it potable

————————

a dying mother's Jesus
obsession, ontological
tank top

————————

his suicide
attempt scooped,
lisping *macher*

————————

he sat
nude on his staircase
only 5'6" yet
aloof, held cane,
avoided being fucked in
quarantine, *Dragnet*
reruns mocking him

————————

   · does a tree
have a secret
911-dialing history, angst
tree, tryst *Selbstmord*?

————————

speculate on river's
extensio—usually
the volcano is mute
or bombed—killed
pharmaceutical rivulets—
a timid basso laugh—
bridge cuts into hill, gives
the hill no quarter, IG Farben

————————

     oratorical skills
of a Moses who got his
ducks all in a row and
God knocked the ducks
over—pork goulash,
whereas chickpeas—
father, smelly
herring, smelts

————————

    forsaken meadow
containing plateau opposites

————————

    my orange
Dixie Cup laughter

————————

    services
tonight but no grim
piety—she Alban Bergs
Liszt, turns him grotty

————————

    or rosy-fingered
Ralph Lauren a Shaker—
or just a Shake 'n Bake
Ralph Lauren—some virile
guys itch their underwear
and talk to themselves

————————

    did I
dream of Joan

Collins? co-star
of a marshmallow?

_____

      conga
line turns Munich
into a tap dance

_____

      no silence
in whale-wreck tree,
a foot stroking itself
in hard shoe

_____

Listerine while I'm
transitioning, TM or tran-
scendental migraine

_____

      a wedge is
taken out of the cloud
to create a replica
of her arm long ago
on dorm bed

———————

he acts bi online but
probably isn't truly bi—
others are bi
in real life but don't
act bi online

———————

internecine
Racine intricate woofer—
I woof a lot, Marschallin-face—
white area of cloud
differentiated surgically
from blue-black area

———————

"Nude River,"
sequel to
"Moon River"

———————

unconscious flowers,
you dominate me
with your intolerable

pink—faceted,
clumped, remorseless

————————

dreamt a dying
charismatic intellectual
gave me a dangerously
sloppy impromptu
haircut in a hilltop mess hall

#47

[psyche luncheonette]

toward the tree
we have an attitude
of a perverted
Best Man who wanders
through the garden
of no volition and
pricks himself
on the thorns of
unwilled movement
through a space
anterior to rehearsal

_____

at age four, appeared
on *Mayor Art,* a TV show—
what role did I play?
Phèdre? Nelson
Eddy as Phèdre?

_____

"right to opacity"
not to be infringed—
difficulty and illegibility
erase the ache

———————

iris, clematis, peony,
geranium, together
momentarily—bird
attempts repeatedly
to build nest in
defunct mailbox

———————

Pearl, a guy—
purl a guy—Agway
to buy pearls

———————

L'École Anormale de
Sprechstimme
Contemporaine
a.k.a.
the Delphine Seyrig

School of Clown
Consciousness is now
accepting applications

_____

write a dime novel
about a guy named
Matt Medium—
in chapter one
Matt Medium
mansplains
to Mady Mesplé

_____

my borscht truck's
nebbish identity

_____

Mary Astor's inaudible "r"
in *The Great Lie*—
"Operator, I want
to make a potty-to-
potty call"

_____

language, mute,
sides with things—
escape language's
confinement by
resembling the thing

———————

barn door rectangles
at angled remove
from mechanical
fence-slat crisscross

———————

birdsong's "charp-quawk"—
other bird's U-shaped call
a dip in the cry, lowering
and then rising—
one skeptical bird
tries to intrude

———————

does the remaining poppy
miss its siblings?

———————

birdhouse's two circular
doors, glory holes
for bird entrance

———————

pine tree's prayer-branches

———————

excitement
necessarily pleasant?
asks the lone bird

———————

birds, rarely
close to each other,
keep calling out
to separated kin

———————

append love
to anything neutral
and learn to abide
unnerving neutrality

———————

car-tire starfish-spikes

———————

triangular barn sits
atop fence because fence
decapitates the barn
or else isolates the
barn-head and makes it
seem comestible

———————

a single hair in
the bathroom sink
forms a momentary
figure eight—
I wash it (wish it?)
down the drain

———————

redemption found
in overlapping shapes I see
despite failure to note
each configuration
permanently—imbibe
their conjunction

_____

remove
pubic centrality
but leave hair
discourse (as
philosophy) intact

_____

psyche luncheonette

_____

with a sense
of foreboding I asked
locals where I could get
a decent Wiener Schnitzel

_____

Judy
(Jew-dy) Garland
in *Judgment at Nuremberg*
is the film's closest
equivalent to a Jew—
marred Monty Clift also
spectrally (by inference)
a Jew

––––––––––

what I called red
flowers on a tree
are actually dead
leaves that turned
permanent orange

––––––––––

hydrangea's pink is
touched or influenced
by yellow, white, green,
and blue—pink
tranquilizes the rival
colors and exists
in a parallel envious
sphere

––––––––––

how
the yellow (approaching
green) accompanies
pink is a long story

––––––––––

dreamt Isabelle
Huppert or Renata
Scotto proposed marriage
to me—gave me 24 hours to decide—
the *New York Times,* covering
the proposal, called me
a social climber

———————

unrehearsed, I perform
in a play (*Wizard of Oz?*)
though no one gave
me a script

———————

          no sentient
cupcake thanks
me—servile
we thank the comatose cupcake

———————

as if the cupcake
were an essay
on music and philosophy

————

a vacuum cleaner—
pink, poignant, small—
leaning unloved
against a hallway wall

#48

[bread and lipstick]

born with
umbilical cord
tied around neck

_____

    mind shattered
into sex-focused pieces—
no release
from libidinal prison

_____

    imagine
Silone wrote
Bread and Lipstick and
De Sica filmed it
and Anjelica Huston
starred in the remake

_____

    angry
at me for ordering

anchovies before she
arrived

————————

      fried donuts
greasy in paper bag,
brought over by
block lady's daughter—
rum cookies rolled
in powdered sugar—
daughter rushing them
over like Pony Express

————————

empty test tube on
S.F. sidewalk—
window mannequin's
dirty bare feet—
pink apartment building
with white frilled
faux-marble doorway
arch on hill I'm
climbing, stopping to
write these words

————————

words intaglioed on
pale blue stucco seashell

_____

vaping genderqueer boi
with yellow socks

_____

      quickly dismissing
the other because the
other doesn't pass muster—
I'm the other who doesn't
pass muster

_____

rusticated brick building
alone leans on its stone mate

_____

      queen never
coughs in public—royal
etiquette a variety
of kosher

_____

he called my
painting "stupid"—
a compliment?

—————

in casket
mother missing
a hand

—————

he will be
picked up by Adam
ánd I will endure
witnessing the pickup

—————

"femmes to the front
of the line," an invitation
not oft issued

—————

your
Swan Lake hospice
Talmud crevice

———————

compulsively frigging
her hair as she
scrolls through Tinder

———————

deleterious to be grandpa
in elevator

———————

ruining the country and no
way to stop him

———————

      lunch
worthless at deli
Iliad and *Odyssey* and endless
revision on her drawstring
strap-on bicameral
consciousness—pallid stubble
ritually reinforced

———————

hotness
a fact not appropriate
to notice or write down

———————

repeatedly I
respond to the thirst
traps who don't see me—
I become (or yearn for)
the graveyard
of not being seen

———————

we ate
horse during the war
in France, force-fed
marriage

———————

nature ode
substandard? what is
achieved or not achieved?
I smell iodine and
hamantaschen

———

autumn's no, spring's
no, winter's maybe,
summer's marquetry

———

her abuse-*moue*,
blurry intolerant tattoo

———

sweet's wool cap temple-
bright, fictive
roses gathered and rent,
water black with
rime, frosty stripes
drumming noncomprehension
into you, same aria,
clobbered
rainstorm *Weltschmerz*

———

nu is Yiddish, grandmother
said *nu* as peddler-joke

———

Billy Budd's madness
on the summer porch
when he repudiates
John Cage and Henry Cowell

———————

      dreamt
sex briefly with
lounge player although
he'd said homophobic
things about me—
his act like Cage or
Antin but sped up,
a violent flip-book

———————

forsaken building
juxtaposed with sky

———————

      refractory
period after a neuron
has been stimulated
and can't receive more

————————

supersaturated—
add one drop
and the solution hardens

————————

    dreamt
obscenely long hair
piled on my head—
attractive young woman
wanted to cut it

————————

repeated fantasy that I
am Joyce Carol Oates

————————

guy who escaped Auschwitz
died—he changed his name
when he arrived in the U.S.—
Shine was the cleaned-up name

————————

windowless yellow truck
radiating contentment
and the Botticelli/Ghirlandaio
library now death-
shadowed because the
friend in that library
with me is now dead—
can you be *now*
dead? if you died
in 2017, then in 2018
are you now dead or
still dead or are you
post-dead? is *dead*
a designation you outgrow?
dead for the day you
die, and the week
afterward, but a
year after your death
you are no longer
a verb—he *is* dead
an impossibility—
he forfeits
the verb of being

————

dreamt Elaine
curated a lipstick art-
show at the Morgan
Library and edited
a collection of Victorian
short stories about lipstick

_____

booming voice on mic
for fraudulent political
or religious cause

_____

but how to insert
a passage in midst
of ongoing flow?

_____

while I clipped your wings
you clipped my wings
and we dove into summer's remains

_____

clutter of drapes doesn't
know how to rebuke me—

eyeglasses dove-
tailing with silver box

_____

await summons from
across-the-street sighing
mother, gesticulating

_____

    chopped chicken liver
as obscene offering,
lifeline—Circean
sgraffiti indecipherable

_____

    no Jews
in my happy library
until the library becomes
unhappy and then I
can bring my Jewish
body into the library's
Hellespont profound

_____

rejected, a pond
containing reflections
not up to pond-par

———————

find cubicles and cubits
of cousinly marvel

———————

Tintoretto's undulant
lines hurt him

———————

to love the foliage
and suspend it from school

———————

discus thrower's mono-
nucleosis reflecting
a longing Acropolis-like

———————

wrinkles on reflected pond
surface cheated of food

———————

crushed grass
upgrowing calm
candy in opus
gleaned from his
civil war

———————

Gunsmoke
its own penis-intertext,
stuffed-sock simulacrum
with fake address, and
I mention her nearness
to Sally Field, how
easily I could become
friends with Sally Field
but not with Robin
Williams or Toshiro
Mifune in *High and Low*

———————

mad
grass of human picnic
basket, his ignored

468

voice I shun
because he won't kink me,
won't choose me as kink
center, will ignore my
kink for two months—
transliterated kink
gradus ad Parnassum

———————

      it hurts
to love *sempiternal*—
like childbirth or when
big square face on
short ideal career-body
unmarries me

———————

I love to disappear—
not red gloves or
shoes or forgetting
red shoes, in sweater
arising a hill, not in
awe of hill I
stand beneath, as if

this were the grass
ending, or the weeding
wedding—weed
the bride, weed
the groom, and become
a swollen mountain
changeling monster
child Harlequin he
knows I know

———————

calm bones near already
spied and already lauded
house, suck house
in trouble-cleft of
protected sex-privacy—
to be not private and not
"him" or crested

———————

ballast the dog bladder
though the dog is
unloved cardboard—
amused at feedback

loop of smeared interiority
loudmouthed upon the
flood but not admitting
the purple can compose
a flood, overly emphatic
green oxide in bottom half-circle
praised for its
strangeness—green
demi-circle lauded
for being the wrong
green, the more
conventionally beautiful
colors gathered in
the north rectangle—
and a gloomier yellow
in cubes rests upon
a happier yellow—
without claiming
the misbegotten yellow
is hieroglyph or
dental reticulation
on a building's Greek
face passed while feeling
a premonition of
yesterday's earthquake

———

you can't have a premonition
of a past event, you can
have a recollection,
refusal, or reversal

———

        yet the earthquake
continues to distract
the mind from objects more
stationary and worth
perpetual regard, the slow
stare that repudiates
haste, the steady glance
you give a rock
or tree—though
trees undergo
metamorphosis and
erosion not suspected
by we who rehearse
but never repair

———

to turn recrimination
inside out and find

the forsaken minim, mute
or speaking, within
rebuke's cold casing

_____

dreamt
I collaborated with Judy
Garland on a documentary

_____

my task was to supply her
with lamb tidbits to clutch

_____

but I missed my cue,
and she fumbled in vain
for the missing lamb fragments

Acknowledgments

I wish to thank the editors of the following publications (print and online), in which portions of this book, sometimes in different versions, appeared:

ARC: The Dirty Issue (Royal College of Art, London):
    "#35 [unseen ultramarine]"
BathHouse Journal: "#40 [her favorite antidepressant
    is tofu]"
Berkeley Poetry Review: "#8 [pumpkin childbirth],"
    "#9 [more kink per square inch please]"
Fence: "#3 [speedy fruit with bubbles]"
The Georgia Review: "#16 [kindergarten emergency
    taproot tableaux]," "#20 [the unguent list]"
Mantis: "#2 [do-it-yourself placenta]"
Modern Queer Poets, ed. Richard Porter (Pilot Press):
    "#4 [egg hat]"
-normal: "#6 [art's marsupial pouch]"
Spine (Ortega y Gasset Projects, Space Sisters Press,
    2018): "#1 [my prostate a shopping mall]"

*

I offer deepest gratitude to Stephen Motika, valiant editor and publisher, for believing in my trance trilogy and seeing it through to completion. Thank you as well to Gia Gonzales, Lindsey Boldt, Caelan Ernest Nardone, and everyone at Nightboat Books, for steering this book into tangible existence. Thank you to Alexa Punnamkuzhyil, for scrutinizing the manuscript. Thank you to Jeff Clark, for exquisite design. Thank you to PJ Mark, for guidance, kindness, solidarity. And thank you to all the writers and artists around me, far and near, who remind me of the rudiments and the fine points.

Wayne Koestenbaum—poet, critic, novelist, artist, performer—has published twenty-one books, including *The Cheerful Scapegoat, Figure It Out, My 1980s & Other Essays, The Anatomy of Harpo Marx, Humiliation, Hotel Theory, Circus, Andy Warhol, Jackie Under My Skin*, and *The Queen's Throat* (nominated for a National Book Critics Circle Award). *Ultramarine* completes his trance trilogy; the first two volumes, also published by Nightboat, are *The Pink Trance Notebooks* and *Camp Marmalade*. In 2020 he received an American Academy of Arts and Letters Award in Literature. His literary archive is at Yale's Beinecke Rare Book and Manuscript Library. He is a Distinguished Professor of English, French, and Comparative Literature at the City University of New York Graduate Center.

Nightboat Books

Nightboat Books, a nonprofit organization, seeks to develop audiences for writers whose work resists convention and transcends boundaries. We publish books rich with poignancy, intelligence, and risk. Please visit our website, www.nightboat.org, to learn about our titles and how you can support our future publications.

The following individuals have supported the publication of this book. We thank them for their generosity and commitment to the mission of Nightboat Books:

Kazim Ali, Anonymous (4), Abraham Avnisan, Jean C. Ballantyne, The Robert C. Brooks Revocable Trust, Amanda Greenberger, Rachel Lithgow, Anne Marie Macari, Elizabeth Madans, Elizabeth Motika, Thomas Shardlow, Benjamin Taylor, Jerrie Whitfield & Richard Motika

This book is made possible, in part, by grants from the New York City Department of Cultural Affairs in partnership with the City Council and the New York State Council on the Arts Literature Program.